OTHER BOOKS BY TRAILER LIFE

An RVer's Annual: The Best of Trailer Life and Motorhome
Edited by Rena Copperman

This collector's edition of the best travel, technical, personality, and feature articles from past issues of the magazines, acknowledged as the leading publications in the RV field, is topped off with a special "Constitution" feature, recalling the recent nationwide anniversary celebration in prose and pictures. Beautiful four-color photos throughout . . . a great gift idea.
8½×11, 208 pages
$15.95 ISBN: 0-934798-21-4

Full-time RVing: A Complete Guide to Life on the Open Road
Bill and Jan Moeller

The answers to all the questions anyone who dreams of traveling full time in an RV may have can be found in this remarkable new source book. *Full-time RVing* takes the mystery out of fulltiming and makes it possible to fully enjoy this once-in-a-lifetime experience.
7¼×9¼, 352 pages
$14.95 ISBN: 0-934798-14-1

RX for RV Performance & Mileage
John Geraghty and Bill Estes

In 32 chapters, this book covers everything an owner must know about how an engine (particularly a V-8) works, vehicle maintenance, propane and diesel as alternative fuels, eliminating engine "ping," improving exhaust systems and fuel economy, and much more.
7¾×9¼, 359 pages
$14.95 ISBN: 0-934798-08-0

The Good Sam RV Cookbook
Edited by Beverly Edwards and the editors of *Trailer Life*

Over 250 easy and delicious recipes, including 78 prize-winners from Good Sam Samboree cook-offs around the country. Also contains tips, ideas, and suggestions to help you get the most from your RV galley.
7¼×9¼, 252 pages
$14.95 ISBN: 0-934798-17-6

These books are available at fine bookstores everywhere. Or, you may order directly from Trailer Life. For each book ordered, simply send us the name of the book, the price, plus $2 per book for shipping and handling (California residents please add 6½% sales tax). Mail to:

Trailer Life Books, P.O. Box 4500, Agoura, CA 91301

You may call our Customer Service representatives if you wish to charge your order or if you want more information. Please phone, toll-free, Monday through Friday, 7:00 A.M. to 6:00 P.M.; Saturday, 7:30 A.M. to 12:30 P.M. Pacific Time, **1-800-234-3450.**

RVing America's Backroads:

Buddy Mays

…Light-hearted I take to the open road,
Healthy, free, the world before me,
The long brown path before me leading
wherever I choose."

Walt Whitman, *Song of the Open Road*

Trailer Life Books
Agoura, California

Trailer Life Book Division

President: Richard Rouse
Vice President/General Manager: Ted Binder
Vice President/Publisher, Book Division: Michael Schneider
General Manager, Book Division: Rena Copperman
Assistant Manager, Book Division: Cindy Lang

Cover design: Bob Schroeder
Cover photograph: Buddy Mays
Interior design: David Fuller/Robert S. Tinnon
Color consultant: almazangraphics
Color separations: Western Laser
Production manager: Rena Copperman
Production coordinator: Robert S. Tinnon
Editorial assistant: Martha McCarty
Indexer: Barbara Wurf
Maps: EarthSurface Graphics

All photographs are the author's unless otherwise credited.

This book was set in ITC Garamond Book by Andresen's Tucson
Typographics and printed on 60-pound Consoweb Brilliant by
R.R. Donnelley and Sons in Willard, Ohio.

ISBN 0-934798-23-0

Library of Congress Cataloging-in-Publication Data

Mays, Buddy
  RVing America's backroads: Texas.

  Includes index.
  1. Automobiles—Texas—Touring. 2. Recreational vehicles—
Texas 3. Texas—Description and travel—1981—   —Guide-
books. I. Title.
GV1024.M39 1989   917.64   88-24798
ISBN 0-934798-23-0

Contents

ACKNOWLEDGMENTS

My thanks to the makers of Foretravel and Winnebago motorhomes, both of whom were kind enough to loan me the best they had while this book was in progress. A special thanks to Rena Copperman, undoubtedly the most enthusiastic and amiable editor a writer could ever work with. And finally, a whole bunch of thanks to the residents of Texas, without whom this meager contribution to travel literature would never have been possible.

Preface

When the editors at TL Enterprises in Agoura, California, asked me to create a book about traveling the backroads of Texas—a book written especially for RVers—frankly, my first thoughts were pessimistic. I knew from experience that excluding interstate highways and metropolitan arteries, *most* of the roads in Texas are back . . . back here, back there, out back, way back, back of beyond . . . you get the idea. Nonetheless the project sounded enjoyable and, massive as it seemed, I accepted on the condition that I alone would choose the highways and byways about which I would write.

My initial research, basically the task of selecting a group of backroad adventures, suitable for RVers from the standpoint of accessibility, scenic beauty, and above all traveler interest, progressed quite nicely. I mapped and plotted for several weeks, steering clear of the usual research sources (tourist officials, press releases, and standard Texas guidebooks—all of which sound more or less alike), gleaning my information from other wellsprings instead. Who better should know about off-the-beaten-track highways, for instance, than the folks who utilize them, people like truckers, farmers, possum hunters, catfishermen, moonshiners, and of course, other RVers.

Once my varicus routes were on paper, the next step was the "proof" stage of the project—an extended motorhome journey through the Lone Star State to confirm or deny the validity of my choices. The trip went smoothly (or relatively so), and several months later, though certainly not an expert on Texas, I had learned enough about the state to feel comfortable in writing my adventures down. The fruit of that labor fills the following pages, and though the sheer magnitude of the logistic material with which I had to deal was mind-boggling to a simple country boy, *RVing America's Backroads: Texas,* was undoubtedly the most enjoyable and enlightening project I've ever undertaken. I can only hope that you, the reader, will have as much fun using this book as I had in its creation.

TEXAS

Texas is one of those rare places where everything always seems a little larger than life, and its vast network of criss-crossing backroads is certainly not expected. As one truck-driving friend told me, "Some of them roads start on one side of the state, kinda pass the middle of nowhere on the way, and end up over yonder on the other side." That of course holds true in other states, but don't forget that Texas is more than a thousand miles across in some places.

The Lone Star State is one of the most beautiful and heterogeneous regions in America, and though the uninitiated may think it is just a vast expanse of flat, barren prairie, believe me it isn't. The eastern part of the state, for example, is as heavily forested as the thick hilly woodlands of New England. In South Texas, sandwiched between lush cattle country and the long, shining Gulf Coast beaches, are virtually millions of acres of swamp, salt marsh, and mesquite-dotted meadows. Then there are the towering desert peaks and canyon-incised "badlands" of the west, the famous Lake District of the north, and the lovely oak- and flower-blanketed Hill Country in the middle.

The people of Texas are heterogeneous and beautiful, too, especially that sixty percent of the population who live and work along the state's backroads. The kind of folks I'm talking about are men like Jake Fullerton, a South Texas ranch cowboy who virtually called out the National Guard when I buried my rig up to the rear axle in soft, red mud ("Come on up to the ranch for a beer," Jake said when I finally pulled free of the muck. "I ain't never knowed nobody that carried his house around on his back."). Or Ester Maddock, a middle-aged East Texas farmwife who volunteered to drive me to the nearest service center seventy-five miles away after I cracked a rotor head on my RV ("I only been this way once when I went over to the hardware to buy some nails," she told me sheepishly. "Fact is, I ain't never been no more than forty miles away from home in any direction.").

In retrospect, I'll offer just one piece of advice to those readers planning a Texas visit—the best time not to travel in the Lone Star State is during the summer. Wait for fall when the eastern hardwoods start to turn, or winter when the winds blow mild and pleasant on the coast, or spring when wildflowers blanket the Hill Country like great, colored carpets. Forgive me, Sam Houston, but mid-summer Texas heat, no matter where you are, will shrivel your skin, pop out your eyes, make your hair curl, and fry your brain like an egg in a hot skillet.

BIG BEND COUNTRY

Texas Mountain Trail

*It's extremely difficult to give a stranger a few
casual and general notions about Texas without
appearing to be either dangerously intemperate or
a liar. It is so vast and spectacular that a really
reasonable person can hardly afford to believe
the truth.*

George Sessions Perry,
Texas, a World in Itself

Probably the first thing most visitors notice about the landscape of West Texas is just how large and empty it really is. You can go for miles here without ever seeing another human being. The ice-blue sky seems to go on forever in every direction. Even the horizon looks as though it might be eternally out of reach. As my grandmother used to say, everything in West Texas is "way over yonder."

I began my West Texas sojurn just north of El Paso by paying a short visit to the Texas Tourist Bureau office located just off Interstate 10 (I-10). The young woman staffing the kiosk inside greeted me with a wave and a grin, almost as though I had been the day's sole customer.

"Where ya headin'?" she asked, her West Texas drawl as salient as honey on dry toast. "Wherever it is, I bet I can help."

I outlined my route on the large kiosk Texas map, emphasizing the areas in which I planned to spend more than a day. Ten minutes later, arms piled high with brochures, maps, and RV camping guides, I walked back to my motorhome. I would learn over the next few months that these friendly TTB offices, located at nine major highway entrances to the state and three major tourist cities, are among the most informative and helpful travel-aid stations in the country.

I returned to the interstate and drove into El Paso, a busy metropolis of 500,000 people located on the Rio Grande. I didn't stop, and unless you have an uncontrollable hankering to visit the Mexican border city of Juarez, I recommend passing El Paso by. Road construction seems to be a fact of life on I-10 and many of the city's major arteries. Add to that a network of narrow streets, unbelievable downtown congestion, and an outdated traffic-light system, and you have a city not made for RVers.

If you do decide to visit Juarez, you can take the well-marked Juarez exit off I-10 (Exit 22 B) south to the border, then straight across the Rio Grande to the *Pronaf.* One of the city's largest shopping centers, this sprawling complex of shops, restaurants, and glass-blowing factories has offered many an impulse buyer a chance at instant gratification. There's plenty of parking at the *Pronaf,* but before crossing the Mexican border make sure you have *in possession* either a vehicle title or letter from your bank stating that you have permission to take your RV out of the United States. Chances are you won't need either but occasionally customs officials make spot checks at the border station. They are extremely particular these days about who drives what across the Rio Grande.

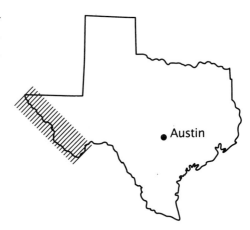

Tour 1 221 miles

DAVIS MOUNTAINS • McDONALD OBSERVATORY • FORT DAVIS • DAVIS MOUNTAINS STATE PARK • PLAINS OF MARFA • SHAFTER • FORT LEATON STATE HISTORICAL SITE • EL CAMINO DEL RIO • TERLINGUA • BIG BEND NATIONAL PARK

Davis Mountains

Interstate 10 east from El Paso isn't one of the state's prettiest highways, but as it leaves the fields and fence rows of the Rio Grande Valley and begins a long, slow climb into the Quitman and Wylie mountains the

Docile Rio Grande.
Near the town of Lajitas, the "Great River" flows quietly along the U.S.–Mexican border.

Rugged and Beautiful.
Sixty miles long and forty miles wide, the Davis Mountains are the most extensive mountain range in Texas.

Texas has ninety-one mountains a mile or more high, all of them located in the Trans-Pecos region. Guadalupe Peak at 8,749 feet is the highest, more than 2,000 feet higher than Mount Mitchell in North Carolina, the highest elevation east of the Mississippi.

vistas become quite spectacular. Writer George Sessions Perry made not-so-subtle note of this region of lost horizons, dry rocky hills, and cactus-covered desert in his book, *Texas, a World in Itself.* "Here," wrote Perry, "is where Texas travels farthest west and then dies of thirst."

I didn't poke about on the long straight road, and three hours and 158 miles later, I left I-10 at the town of Kent and turned south onto State Route (SR) 118. Within a few miles I entered the foothills of the Davis Mountains, once home to marauding bands of Apache and Comanche Indians, and disreputably known to early pioneers as the "badlands of Texas."

Sixty miles in length and about forty wide, the Davis Mountains are the state's most expansive range. Beautiful any time of year, the softly rolling hills and stubby peaks are especially lovely in late autumn when the summer heat has dissipated and the emory oak and scrub juniper are cool and glowing in their pre-winter foliage. SR 118, which bisects the mountains north to south, is narrow and twisty in places, but highway shoulders are wide, giving RVers plenty of room to pull over when the situation demands. In my case, I stopped a number of times to observe and photograph wild animals that seemed to be as profuse as flowers along the road. In one instance, a small herd of javelina (also called peccary or wild pig) meandered across the pavement. In another, a white-tailed buck, glorious in November coat and antlers, leaped over the highway fence, ambled across the road, and posed for a few moments on the shoulder while I took his picture. It seemed as if desert quail scurried from every bush; on one low hill a golden eagle warily leered from his perch in an ancient juniper. On a good day, I thought to myself as I slowly negotiated the winding highway, driving through the Davis Mountains is like driving through a private zoological garden.

McDonald Observatory

Thirty miles south of Kent, SR 118 begins a steep and steady climb upward. A few miles farther on, I turned left on a paved side road and followed the signs to the world-famous McDonald Observatory.

Built in 1932 and perched atop the summit of Mount Locke at an altitude of 6,800 feet, McDonald is one of the best situated such institutions in America. Clear air, a high ratio of cloudless nights, and its distance from any concentration of artificial light, say astronomers, have made the isolated station a stargazer's heaven. The original 82-inch reflector telescope constructed here provided scientists with an almost unbelievable magnification of distant stars and planets. Then in 1968 a far more powerful 107-inch reflector was built at McDonald, offering an even better view of the universe. Today astronomers from all over the world visit the Davis Mountains to utilize the observatory's phenomenal research facilities.

Wild Pig?
Not really. Javelina or peccaries, quite common in this portion of Texas, are related not to pigs, but to hippopotami.

Mountaintop Star Watch.
Situated atop lofty Mount Locke, McDonald Observatory is visited by astronomers from all over the world.

Desert Pincushion.
The daggerlike leaves of this Davis Mountain agave make it difficult for cattle or deer to feed on the plant's tender young shoots.

At the W. L. Moody Jr. Visitor Center located at the foot of Mount Locke, you'll find informative audiovisual programs about McDonald's scientific programs as well as the area's natural history. Guided tours of the site are offered each day, September through May at 2 P.M., and June through August at 9:30 A.M. and 2 P.M. Tours take about an hour and are highlighted by a visit to the massive reflector telescope housed in its white mountain-top dome. On Tuesday and Saturday evenings, visitors can attend "Star Parties" at the observatory (make your reservations in advance), where they can examine the heavenly bodies through portable but powerful telescopes set up by the staff.

The two-mile road from W. L. Moody Jr. Visitor Center to the main observatory site is steep and narrow but passable for automobiles and small- to medium-sized RVs. I do suggest, however, that if your rig is thirty feet or longer in length you park at the visitor center and hitch a ride to the top with another motorist. There's a small turnaround area on the mountain just below the smaller dome, but if you miss it and traffic is heavy, turning around can be difficult. If you can't catch a ride, walk to the top. Panoramic views of the Davis Mountains are breathtaking from almost anywhere along the road.

One last suggestion: If you want to attend an evening Star Party but don't like the idea of driving back into Fort Davis at night, there's a lovely roadside picnic area just a few miles north of the observatory on SR 118. The place doesn't have water or hookups, but it's hidden in a thick copse of grey oak on the south side of the highway and is pleasingly private. I've passed the site a dozen times and have yet to see it occupied by more than a few vehicles.

Fort Davis

After an interesting tour of the visitor center and observatory, and a few extra minutes spent admiring the superb mountain view, I left McDonald to the eagles, rejoined SR 118, and drove the sixteen miles to the historic West Texas town of Fort Davis.

A long and colorful history surrounds this little community. During the mid-1800s, as pioneers and gold hunters began to push westward in search of land and riches, many fell prey to hostile bands of Indians that roamed the West Texas region at will. The problem was especially severe along the Overland Trail that spanned the 600 miles of wilderness between San Antonio and El Paso. Then in 1854 the U.S. Army established Fort Davis, manning it with twelve full companies of cavalry troops and infantry. It was the first military outpost to guard the Overland Trail and was eventually responsible for saving thousands of lives.

Today the town boasts a population of 900 and is popular with RVers and other visitors because of its mild winter climate and dramatic mountain scenery. Downtown architecture resembles that of an old western town, and there are a number of small galleries and museums in which visitors can browse. The Neill Musuem, located in the historic old True-

Where Cavalry Trod.
Laid out fortress-style around a wide, central parade ground, Fort Davis National Historic Site is one of the best preserved of the state's frontier forts.

heart House, is seven blocks west of the county courthouse and features early-Texas toys, dolls, and furniture. Another showcase of pioneer culture in Fort Davis is the Overland Trail Museum, also located in the downtown area. On display here are numerous ranch and law enforcement artifacts as well as tools and implements used by Overland Trail travelers.

Fort Davis National Historic Site

For me the main attraction at Fort Davis is the old fort itself, located just south of the SR 118 and SR 17 junction. Partially restored and operated as a visitor attraction by the National Park Service, this once omnipotent military outpost is well worth a close inspection if you're interested in the life and times of the western frontier.

As it was originally, the post today is laid out fortress-style around a wide, flat, central parade ground. To the west, toward the wide mouth of a canyon, is Officer's Row, a baker's dozen of reconstructed (circa 1850) homes in which the fort's small complement of cavalry and infantry officers once resided. To the north are post headquarters, the chapel, cemetery, and guard house. The enlisted men's barracks, commissary, stables, and corrals are on the east side of the parade grounds. The visitor center and administration building lie on the south end of the main barracks.

A number of hiking trails meander through the fort and surrounding hills; the most scenic one begins at the north end of Officer's Row and winds onto an overlooking ridge above the post. The park service offers guided tours of the fort throughout the day, and an audiovisual program

Tougher than an Old Boot.
This ancient structure on the grounds of Fort Davis has withstood more than a hundred years of wind and weather.

Stone Sentinels.
Eroded stone monoliths stand guard in
the Davis Mountains near old Fort Davis.

in the visitor center operates continually. Perhaps the fort's most unique feature is a dramatic on-the-hour sound show—the vivid re-creation of a nineteenth-century military parade complete with bugles, hoofbeats, shouted commands, and the clank and jangle of mounted cavalry in close-order drill. My first visit to the fort occurred just before sundown, and this sensational audio reincarnation made the hair virtually stand up on the back of my neck. Fort Davis is open daily except Christmas from 8 A.M. to 6 P.M. in the summer, and from 8 A.M. to 5 P.M. in the winter.

Davis Mountain State Park

Two or three privately owned RV parks are open on a year-round basis in Fort Davis, but I chose instead to stay at nearby Davis Mountains State Park, nestled in the shady bottom of Keesey Creek Canyon three miles north of town. Camping sites are level with all hookups available, and most access roads are paved. During the summer, state park rangers offer campfire programs each evening that cover local history and Indian lore, as well as the natural history of the Davis Mountains. Hiking trails in the park are numerous (one, the North Ridge Trail, leads to Fort Davis Historical Site), and there's a scenic auto route known as Skyline Drive that slithers along a high ridge overlooking the campground. I found the park an excellent place to stay while exploring the Fort Davis area, but I recommend making advance reservations, at least during late spring when visitor traffic is heaviest.

Plains of Marfa

After two days in Fort Davis, poking around the old cavalry post and the town's shops and museums, I relinquished my snug camping space in the state park and headed south toward the Mexican border.

The stretch of SR 17 from Fort Davis to the ranching town of Marfa runs through a flat, somewhat barren landscape known locally as the Plains of Marfa, or in some cases simply "the Plains." Once a major staging area for Apache and Comanche Indian attacks on travelers using the Overland Trail, today the Plains are owned primarily by prominent cattle ranchers.

Perhaps the most unusual thing about this wide expanse of bunchgrass, agave, rabbit bush, and cactus is its dense population of pronghorn—fleet-footed, deerlike animals better known as American antelope. Before 1850, these cagey critters were the only large North American mammals to

High Plains Drifter.
Fleet-footed pronghorn, also known as American antelope, are common inhabitants of the Marfa Plains.

Plains of Marfa.
Once a major staging area for Apache and Comanche Indians, today these wide grasslands are owned by local ranchers.

even come close in numbers to those of the bison, and at one time uncounted millions roamed the prairies and Great Plains of America.

In the 1870s and 1880s, when domestic livestock began arriving on the scene, however, pronghorn herds rapidly decreased as ranchers and sheepmen slaughtered them mercilessly for both food and sport. By 1905 less than 20,000 remained in the wild and only through a massive conservation effort—sponsored by the U.S. government along with state game and fish organizations—were they saved from the one-way journey to extinction.

Today pronghorn are once again relatively common (they are protected vigorously by local ranchers on the Plains of Marfa), and you'll undoubtedly pass several herds grazing along the highway between Fort Davis and Marfa. As long as you stay inside your vehicle and don't make undue noise, the animals should remain calm and you will be able to photograph them quite easily.

Shafter

At Marfa I picked up US 67 and headed the nose of my rig toward the semi-ghost town of Shafter, once the largest silver mining town in the entire state of Texas, but today little more than a colorful desert ruin.

A century ago, Shafter was known by law enforcement officers as a "hot spot," a roughneck mining town filled with brawlers, hooligans, and prostitutes, and existing solely because of the prodigious deposits of silver ore lying in the surrounding hills. It was also the site of a major Texas race riot, probably the first ever to take place in the western part of the state.

The problems started in 1890 when a Mexican national rode into town, aiming to end the careers of two police officers who had arrested one of his friends. Loaded to the gills with mescal (a powerful Mexican liquor), he was quickly arrested, and because Shafter had no jail, was tied to a tree while awaiting transport to Marfa. Sometime during the night, vigilantes loosened the fellow's bonds, walked him to the edge of town, and simply blew him away.

Because he was a Mexican, the local Mexican community threatened to take revenge and shortly thereafter armed themselves and began to shoot up the town. During the fracas one Texas Ranger was killed and another wounded as they attempted to quell the riot; during the night a number of local citizens were also shot down. Then, just after daylight, fifteen Texas Rangers and several American miners surrounded the Mexicans, told them they were about to make a one-way trip to Hell, and requested they send out the women and kids. Hungover, but not stupid, the Mexicans quickly surrendered.

Today Shafter consists of little more than a few ancient and weathered adobe houses surrounded by decaying stone ruins. It's a good place to have lunch, however, and the old post office and small white Catholic church in the center of town make a memorable photograph silhouetted against the harsh desert background.

White Dove in the Desert.
The small, white Catholic church in Shafter presents a contrasting silhouette against the harsh desert background.

Fort Leaton

In the border town of Presidio, I turned east onto Farm-to-Market Road (FM) 170 and three miles later pulled into the spacious parking lot of Fort Leaton State Historical Site. Located on the banks of the Rio Grande, this old fortress-cum-trading post was built by frontiersman Ben Leaton in 1848 on the main wagon-and-horse trail from Chihuahua, Mexico, to San Antonio, Texas. From here the enterprising Leaton operated a lucrative, if somewhat suspect, business. One week he would supply the wide-ranging U.S. Army patrols who kept the local Indians at bay with food and equipment, and the next he would encourage the same Indians to raid settlements just across the border. Leaton would then trade guns and ammunition for whatever cattle the Indians managed to steal.

More than two dozen of the original forty rooms in the old fort have been restored, and the site presently offers interpretive exhibits about area history and culture and Chihuahuan desert ecology. Eventually the Texas Division of Parks and Wildlife hopes to furnish many of the buildings with frontier-type appointments. There's a shaded picnic area adjacent to the park that provides some nice views of the Rio Grande Valley.

Adobe Abode.
The thick adobe (mud brick) walls of
Fort Leaton once kept out bullets as
well as the intense summer heat.

Wheels West.
This old ox cart, once a primary method
of transportation in west Texas, is on
display at Fort Leaton.

El Camino del Rio

I spent a pleasant hour at Fort Leaton, then turned east on FM 170, following the sinuous bed of the Rio Grande along what locals call the *El Camino del Rio,* Spanish for "the River Road." Slicing through nearly fifty miles of remote mountain and canyon country before it finally begins to flatten out near Terlingua, the River Road, I had been told, was one of the most scenic drives in Texas.

I drove the highway in November and admittedly the scenery was spectacular. To the left the rock-studded peaks and ocotilla-blanketed ridges of the *Sierra Rica* (Rich Mountains) sloped raggedly away northward; on the right lay the green winding snake of the Rio Grande, low and surprisingly clear at this time of year. Along the river's banks, cottonwood trees, willow, tamarisk, and towering thickets of bamboo were just beginning to harmonize into a colorful scarf of red and gold. Bird life along the river was abundant; in just a few miles I spotted both great blue and little brown herons, egrets, Gambel's quail, bright red cardinals, and a legion of ducks, shorebirds, and hawks.

Along the Rio Grande.
El Camino del Rio or "The River Road" is one of the prettiest highways in Texas. Skirting the Sierra Rica on the south, the road follows the winding Rio Grande from Presidio to Lajitas.

Water Vultures.
One of the lesser-known species of migrating waterfowl, cormorants are among the more common birds found in west Texas.

There are a number of primitive but cozy riverbottom campgrounds along El Camino del Rio, most of them created by the large numbers of white-water rafters who float the Rio Grande here in the winter and spring. There are also hazards on the road that every RVer should note. First, although the pavement itself is in good condition, the highway winds and twists through the mountains like a sun-crazy rattlesnake and the going is slow—thirty-five miles per hour or less. Second, from beginning to end the road crosses literally hundreds of small, shallow arroyos, and if it happens to be raining, some may be filled with water. If the weather is wet, I suggest you camp for a day until the danger of flash floods has passed. Moving at speed, a Texas flash flood can sweep a car or motorhome off the road as effortlessly as it moves a small boulder.

And by the way, there is one really nasty grade on this highway to watch out for. Thirty miles east of Presidio, FM 170 elbows sharply upward as it negotiates the summit of a steep-sided east-west ridge. The

Verdant Snake.
The Rio Grande winds its way slowly through the rugged canyon country along the US–Mexican border east of Presidio. The lone ocotilla cactus here seems to grow out of solid rock.

long, slow grade is seven percent both up and down. By the time I reached bottom on the far side my brakes were smoking (even though I had been in low gear), and the sweat was beading on my forehead. It took a brisk walk along the river and a long lunch to convince my legs to finally stop shaking.

Abandoned Terlingua

Prior to 1890, the area around present-day Terlingua was inhabited by only a few Mexican sheepherders and an occasional band of Apache Indians. Dry, hot, and exceedingly barren, the javelina- and rattlesnake-infested landscape was hardly what most early-American pioneers would have called appealing.

Ten years before the century turned, however, cinnabar (a mineral used to make mercury) was discovered in the nearby hills, and within just a few short years Terlingua had erupted into a rough-and-tumble mining town of 2,000. Over the next five decades, virtually thousands of tons of cinnabar were removed from the Terlingua hills. Then in 1946 the bottom fell out of the mercury market and as quickly as it had come, the town disappeared. Hundreds of wooden shacks and stone buildings that had housed so many for so long were left to rot and weather in the desert sun.

Today there's still not much to be found in Terlingua, but some of the old buildings have undergone a facelift, the streets have been graded, and

Remnants of the Past.
An ancient stone and mud building and a rusting automobile offer a glimpse of the past in the semi-ghost town of Terlingua.

a small country store, a river-running outfitter, and a home-style-cooking café are in full operation. One of the café's co-owners is Sarah Whitson, a former managing editor of the highly respected *Texas Monthly* magazine. A slender, attractive woman in her early forties, Sarah is fairly typical of Terlingua's population. "City life was getting old," she told me as I sipped a freshly made cup of coffee in the Terlingua Café, "and so was I."

In 1984, Sarah simply lost interest in the bustle and congestion of Austin. She rented her large, rambling home, packed up her clothes, and moved lock, stock, and frying pan to Terlingua.

"I always loved white-water rafting," she said, "so I cleaned up my Austin act, moved down here, and got a job with the local river-running company. Now I'm doing what I *want* to do, not what I have to do. We don't have a lot here in Terlingua, but a trip back to Austin or any other city shows us just how much we *do* have."

These days Terlingua is best known for its World Championship Chili Cookoff, held on the first weekend of November. Each year more than 5,000 chili lovers from all over the world converge on this small West Texas town, eager to sample the offerings of chili chefs from as far away as Europe and Africa. RVers, of course, are more than welcome. There are no improved accommodations in town, but a large field to the west has been set aside for camping.

Terlingua and nearby Lajitas are also headquarters for a number of white-water rafting organizations, which, if you're interested, will carry you through the canyons of Big Bend National Park to the east. Reservations are needed even for one-day trips because distances traveled to and from the river are so great; groups must often leave before dawn.

Big Bend Country

I joined SR 118 a few miles past Terlingua at the town of Study (pronounced *stoody*) Butte and followed it to the western entrance of Big Bend National Park. My goal for the day was to reach the national park headquarters, located at Panther Junction.

A colossal place is the Big Bend Country, far too imposing to be measured in acres. The earth here is computed in square miles, 1,100 of them to be exact, basted together in a quilt of haphazard loveliness. The morphology is that of desert, physiographically known as Chihuahuan. It is a land of rock and sand, of dagger plants and blue-throated hummingbirds, of mountains and cholla cactus and wild pigs, of rattlesnakes and red-tailed hawks.

The name *Big Bend* refers to the wide *U* that the Rio Grande makes in this portion of West Texas. Indian tribes used to claim that when the Great Spirit finished making the earth, he dumped all the leftover rocks into Big Bend. Spanish explorers called it the "unknown land," and for hundreds of years civilization simply passed it by. Even today, walled in by steep mountain ranges on the north and protected by a series of river canyons on the south, it remains a world apart.

The longest river in the state is the Rio Grande, which forms the international boundary between the United States and Mexico and is 1,248 miles long in Texas alone. Second longest waterway is the Red River, separating Texas from Oklahoma.

Road Guide.
If you plan to explore Big Bend by road, a copy of *Road Guide to Paved and Improved Dirt Roads of Big Bend National Park* is a must.

Officially established in 1944, the park is a vast place that certainly invites exploration, but it can't be seen in a couple of hours. There are more than 100 miles of paved highways here, nearly 200 miles of graded road, and probably more than 1,000 miles of hiking, backpacking, and river trails. Over 1,000 types of plants, 350 species of birds, and 70 different species of mammals are found within park boundaries; the list goes on and on.

Panther Junction

The official hub of activity in Big Bend is the National Park Service's Panther Junction Visitor Center, located at the junction of SR 118 and US 385 in the central part of the park. Here visitors are required to pay an admission fee and also reserve their campsites if they plan to spend the night. A post office, bookstore, gasoline station and small grocery store are all located within the Panther Junction compound adjacent to the interpretive center.

If you plan to stay awhile (the camping limit is fourteen days), pick up a copy of *Road Guide to Paved and Improved Dirt Roads of Big Bend National Park,* available in the bookstore. It's an extremely handy booklet if you want to tour the park in your vehicle. And though there are no improved campgrounds at Panther Junction, if you happen to arrive late you can request a camping site at one of the nearby primitive sites just for the night. I stayed at a place called Government Springs my first evening in Big Bend, and the only company I had was a herd of javelina.

Big Bend Mulies.
Near the edge of Santa Elena Canyon, this duo of mule deer does stand calmly while visitors take their picture. Far tamer than their white-tailed cousins, mulies are one of the park's most common animals.

Santa Elena—Castolon

In my opinion, the most scenic auto route in Big Bend is Santa Elena Drive, a slender ribbon of asphalt that heads southwest to the Rio Grande, bisecting a veritable moonscape of geologic gargoyles and great walled dikes in the process. The road is twenty-two miles long from the point it leaves SR 118 west of Panther Junction to its terminus at Santa Elena Canyon overlook.

At Castolon, a small settlement near road's end, there's a "frontier" store that has picnic supplies, groceries, ice, and some general merchandise. Cottonwood Campground is located just west of Castolon on the Rio Grande. Water, pit toilets, grills, and picnic tables are provided at the thirty-five-site RV-and-tent park, but there are no sewer or electric hookups. A number of short hiking and nature trails begin near the campground, and of course the backpacking options are endless. Backcountry permits are issued free at the Castolon Ranger Station.

The Basin

The paved highway to Basin Campground (known simply as "The Basin") leaves SR 118 about three miles west of Panther Junction and will carry you through the stony heart of the ruggedly beautiful Chisos Mountains. The first few miles of this seven-mile-long road are relatively flat, but the last section is steep and twisty. The park service recommends that RVs and travel trailers more than twenty-three feet long go elsewhere.

A lovely mountain-bound recreation area high in the slopes of the Chisos Peaks, Basin Campground has sixty-five improved sites, but like Cottonwood Campground it provides only water, comfort stations, grills, and picnic tables. You can purchase groceries, beer, picnic supplies, and backpacking and hiking equipment at the Chisos Basin Store located near the campground. Park rangers offer both guided nature walks and evening campfire programs, and hiking trails in the surrounding mountains are numerous. Backcountry permits may be obtained at the Chisos Basin Ranger Station.

Boquillas Canyon—Rio Grande Village

The twenty-mile-long paved road to Boquillas Canyon and Rio Grande Village begins at the Panther Juncton Visitor Center and heads southeast toward the beautiful Sierra del Carmen Mountains. Road's end is at the Rio Grande near the tiny Mexican village of Boquillas.

Rio Grande Village (located on the river) is Big Bend's most popular camping area as well as its largest. You'll find 200 campsites here (water, toilets, grills, picnic tables, and a dump station are provided), and the nearby Rio Grande Village Store has a coin-operated laundry and hot showers as well as groceries, beer, and ice. Evening campfire programs and guided nature hikes are offered daily by park rangers, and several picturesque hiking trails begin near the campground. Backpackers can obtain their free backcountry permits at the Rio Grande Village Ranger Station.

River Trips

Riding a neoprene raft or canoe on the Rio Grande through one or more of the phenomenal Big Bend canyons is an experience you won't soon forget. There are five major chasms separating this little Texas peninsula from the Republic of Mexico, and every one of them is spectacular. To the northwest is Santa Elena, a 23-mile-long limestone box with walls so steep in places the canyon rim cannot be seen from the river bank. Downriver is Mariscal, where the Sierra de San Vicente drop nearly 2,000 vertical feet to the metallic-green river, and where in places the channel itself is unceremoniously squeezed to a width of 5 feet. Below Mariscal are San Vicente and Hot Springs canyons, both short but stunning gashes in the earth's crust, and last is Boquillas—longest of them all—snaking its way through the Sierra Del Carmen for nearly 30 miles.

Boquillas, especially, holds fond memories for me since it was there a few years ago—along with my friend Mary and a faithful but overeager springer spaniel named Boomer—that I made my first lengthy canoe trip.

Careful research (a look at a Texas road map and a few frank questions put to the owner of a gasoline station in Presidio) had revealed that Boquillas Canyon was not an overly dangerous stretch of the Big Bend country. There were no rapids of consequence, we understood, just thirty miles of gurgling pools and long, silent reaches of gentle, insouciant water. Needless to say, Mary and I were somewhat surprised when after

only an hour on the river, past the concrete picnic tables of Rio Grande Village and a pair of five-year-old señoritas skinny-dipping in the shallows, we hit a large rapid.

It was all over in a second. The white water itself wasn't bad even though we scraped a few times on the rocks, but paddle power alone wasn't strong enough to swing the canoe around an old dead tree that overhung midcurrent. An instant before we hit, Boomer decided he'd seen enough and bailed out over the port side. At the same time, Mary and I reacted automatically and leaned away from the obstacle. Over we went, headfirst with no lifejackets, into deep water.

However, we lived through the ordeal and went on to enjoy one of the most peaceful and pleasant vacations in memory. Not much has changed

Desert Solitude.
Canoeists slowly guide their canoe down
Boquillas Canyon, one of the most dramatic of the great Big Bend chasms.

in Boquillas since a morning long ago when some cave-dwelling *Homo sapiens* wrapped a ragged mammoth hide around his middle, scratched his big toe with a rock, and went out to face the day. The isolation goes on forever; yucca still rattle in the morning wind; the river still gurgles; the surrounding walls still stretch up and out toward a cornflower-blue sky. Four days after our somewhat dubious beginning, we popped out of the canyon at Adams Ranch, caught a ride back to our car, retrieved the canoe and gear, and headed home.

There wasn't much in the way of professional outfitters in Big Bend when we made that first trip, but today white-water rafting organizations are based at Lajitas, Terlingua, and in the town of Marathon, forty miles north of the park. Most outfitters furnish everything you'll need except personal clothing and offer trips as short as a few hours or as long as a week. Costs range from $100 to $250 per person per day, depending upon the trip length. You can still run the canyons on your own if you wish, assuming you have the equipment and experience, plus a special permit issued free by the park service. An excellent mile-by-mile river guide is for sale at the Panther Junction bookstore.

I have friends who claim that everything in Big Bend either bites, stings, or eats human flesh. But after spending three full days in the park revisiting old haunts, wandering the trails, and exploring backroads that I hadn't driven on earlier trips, I can truthfully say that this massive expanse of desert terrain is one of the wildest and most beautiful reserves in North America. I'll also guarantee that if you aren't already a desert rat, a lover of all things hot, prickly, and covered with rocks, a few days in Big Bend will quickly remedy that condition.

POINTS OF INTEREST: Texas Tour 1

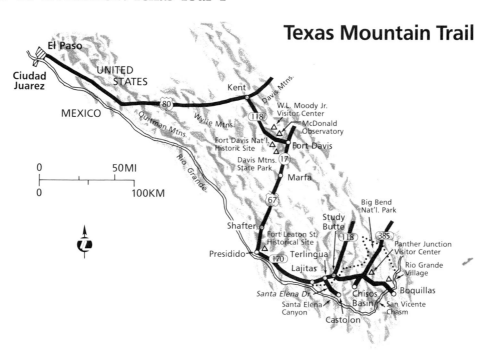

Texas Mountain Trail

ACCESS: From El Paso, take *I-10* east; south on *SR 118* at Kent.

INFORMATION: *Fort Davis Chamber of Commerce,* Fort Davis, TX, 79734, (915) 426-3015; *McDonald Observatory,* P.O. Box 1337, Fort Davis, TX 79734, (915) 426-3263; *Big Bend National Park,* Superintendent, Big Bend National Park, TX, (915) 477-2251.

ANNUAL EVENTS:

Terlingua: *The World Championship Chili Cookoff,* held first weekend in November.

MUSEUMS:

Fort Davis: *Neill Museum,* June–September, 9 A.M. to 5 P.M., admission, featuring antique toys, dolls, furniture; *Overland Trail Museum,* open Wednesday through Sunday afternoons, summer, admission, featuring antiques and artifacts from pioneer days.

OUTFITTERS:

Big Bend National Park: *Outback Expeditions,* P.O. Box 44, Terlingua, TX 79852, (915) 371-2490; *Big Bend River Tours,* Box 317, Lajitas, TX 79852, (915) 424-3219.

RESTAURANTS:

Fort Davis: *Sutler's Restaurant,* Historic Limpia Hotel, Mexican-American food.

Terlingua: *Terlingua Café,* country-style, home-cooked food, Tuesday–Saturday, 8 A.M. to 2 P.M., Sunday and Monday, 8 A.M. to 10 P.M.

BORDER SOJOURN
West Texas

The Texas border is about a thousand miles long,
counting detours, and it's just as wide as anybody
who owns a cow over there thinks it is.

Houston Post, 1910

The segment of rugged West Texas terrain lying along the Mexican border has always intrigued me. One of the American Southwest's richest areas, not in precious stones or minerals (though they are abundant as well), but in history and tradition, little has changed here in the past century. The landscape, except in the few towns and small cities, is nearly uninhabited, and driving along the roads, motorists are as likely to see a coyote or a cowboy as another automobile. Gasoline stations, motels, RV parks, and other contrivances of our modern and mobile society are sometimes as rare as teeth on a chicken.

I toured this region in early December, after the devastating summer heat had subsided to tolerable levels, and just as the desert foliage was beginning to reveal a delicate autumn tint. It's a perfect time of year to explore the border country, almost as good as mid-spring when newly bloomed wildflowers have transformed the roadside and adjacent hills into a haphazard quilt of many colors.

I'll warn you ahead of time that there aren't many visitor attractions in this part of Texas, at least not the kind you can visit for thirty minutes, buy a postcard or hamburger, then go on your way. The main appeal here for most RVers is the comeliness and isolation of the land itself. Secondary is the subtle "frontier" aura that clings like a historic, ghostly mist to the border country and its inhabitants. Offering perfect examples of both is the town of Langtry, nestled in rocky desert near the Rio Grande, 120 miles east of Marathon. Born in sweat, soaked in blood, and steeped in fable, this tiny rural community—once the home of the legendary Judge Roy Bean—was the perfect place to start my border sojourn.

*Tour **2** 238 miles*

LANGTRY • PECOS RIVER • SEMINOLE CANYON STATE HISTORICAL SITE • AMISTAD RECREATION AREA • DEL RIO • CIUDAD ACUNA • EAGLE PASS • PIEDRAS NEGRAS • LAREDO • NUEVO LAREDO

The Law West of the Pecos

I paused long enough in Marathon to fill my rig's gasoline tanks, then headed east on US 90. Three hours later I turned south onto Loop 25, negotiated the mile or so of winding pavement to Langtry, and parked in the spacious lot in front of the Judge Roy Bean Visitor Center. There's a Texas Tourist Bureau office in the same building, so if you're short of maps and information stop here first.

Langtry began as a railroad town, one of hundreds of similar communities on the West Texas frontier founded to feed, house, and entertain the men who were slowly but steadily stitching America together with steel. Like its neighbors, Langtry was little more than a tent city, according to one frontier scribe, "a half-baked collection of canvas shelters that leaked when it rained and provided just enough privacy so that scorpions could scurry about the floors without being heard."

Because of its isolation and very nature, Langtry was virtually lawless. Besides a hundred or so rough-and-tumble railroad workers who were

Past and Present.
The border areas of Texas are cowboy country, but you can never tell what they will be riding. Here, a horseman and helicopter-borne cowboy meet at dawn to discuss the day's workload.

Law West of the Pecos.
Seated in the Jersey Lily Saloon, Judge Roy Bean provided a swift and colorful brand of justice that would make him famous over the next two decades.

Wind Power.
Overlooking the small town of Langtry, this old windmill once provided well water for humans and cattle alike.

always eager to let off steam, it was teeming with gamblers, thieves, prostitutes, and outlaws. By 1882, violence in the streets was so routine that railroad officials asked for help from the Texas Rangers. Immediately a contingent of officers was transferred to Langtry from nearby Del Rio, and to dispense the rangers' law, a justice of the peace was appointed by the state.

The new judge was Roy Bean, a former storekeeper in the neighboring tent town of Vinegaroon, owner of a pet bear named Bruno, and a smart, quick-witted man who, uniquely for the times, had somehow developed a code of ethics. Seated in his Jersey Lily Saloon (named for English actress Lillie Langtry, whom Bean admired) with an 1879 edition of the *Revised Statutes of Texas* in his hand, Bean provided a swift and colorful brand of justice that would make him famous over the next two decades as "the law west of the Pecos." For instance, contrary to legend, Bean never sentenced anyone, even murderers, to hang. Instead, the worst criminals were relieved of their horses, money, and guns, then simply expelled from town. Alone and on foot in terrain nicknamed "Hell's Half Acre" by railroad men, lawbreakers would have found it preferable had they gone instead to the gallows.

Bean died of a heart attack in 1903 but his legend—a combination of fact, fiction, and fancy— has survived the test of time, a book or two, and several movies. Langtry, on the other hand (named by the way for a civil engineer and not Lillie Langtry), wasn't so lucky. Today it is a tiny place, home to maybe fifteen families, a gasoline station, and a couple of small, unshaded RV parks that cater mainly to big-game hunters. The hub of the community is the Judge Roy Bean Visitor Center, located in the middle of town. Encompassed on its spacious grounds is the old Jersey Lily Saloon, a small museum that exhibits many of Roy Bean's belongings, a botanical garden, and a self-guided nature walk. I heartily recommend stopping at this town since it was here that a good portion of old-west history was made. The visitor center and museum are open 8 A.M. to 5 P.M. every day of the year except Christmas.

Pecos River Canyon

Driving east from Langtry on US 90, it was easy for me to see why empty-handed expulsion would have been a fate worse than death for trouble-makers who faced Judge Roy Bean. Crisscrossed by deep, impassable limestone canyons, the cactus-blanketed, rattlesnake-infested terrain is so rugged and inhospitable that only the hardiest of men could have survived for more than a few days.

Fifteen miles from town, the largest and deepest of the canyons cradles the Pecos River in its maw. Today a long, steel bridge spans the chasm,

Cradle of Green Water.
The Pecos River canyon, east of Langtry, is one of the region's most inspiring sights. This viewpoint is on US 90, fifteen miles from town.

and if you want to stop for pictures there's a paved parking area just past the bridge's easternmost abutment. I drove over the river in early afternoon, and the combination of emerald-green water and plunging limestone and lava cliffs was a spectacular sight. For an even better view of the region, you can drive on past the bridge a few hundred feet and turn south to a hilltop picnic area overlooking the river. It's a great place to eat lunch and stretch, and free-of-charge, overnight camping is permitted. A number of trails lead from the picnic site down to the canyon lip, and at least one meanders into the backcountry via the east canyon rim.

Seminole Canyon State Historical Park

I spent an hour on the Pecos exploring and taking pictures before heading east again, but I had no sooner returned to US 90 when I spotted a sign on the south side of the highway pointing the way to Seminole Canyon State Historical Park. The place wasn't on my map, and surprisingly, there was no mention whatsoever of a Seminole Canyon in the Texas guidebook I carried.

I found the park's small but modern visitor center a quarter-mile from the highway, perched like a vulture on the canyon rim. Inside, a friendly ranger took my $2 admission fee and informed me that the 2,100-acre park and adjacent canyon were both named for a group of Oklahoma Indians that roamed the area during the 1800s. He also said it was one of the least visited historical sites in the state, probably because of its remote location.

There are some interesting geologic and early-man exhibits in the visitor center museum, and at Fate Bell Shelter, an ancient camping site in the canyon itself, are a set of 8,000-year-old Indian pictographs. Archaeologists claim the Fate Bell rock paintings are the oldest such illustrations in North America. They are well worth seeing but be warned that the hike into the canyon is strenuous and that visitors have to be accompanied by a park ranger. Guided tours take place Wednesday through Sunday and leave the visitor center at 10 A.M. and 3 P.M. sharp. I suggest carrying a canteen of water and wearing sturdy boots if you decide to make the trek.

Seminole Canyon camping area is located just south of the visitor center, and it's a great place to spend a day or two while exploring the country. The site has no hookups but there are shelters, picnic tables, cooking grills, and some magnificent views of the surrounding canyon country. For really active hikers, a six-mile-round-trip hiking trail starts near the camping area and ends at a scenic overlook on the Rio Grande. Again, the walk is strenuous but the views are worth the effort.

Amistad Recreation Area

Water began to back up in Amistad Lake in May, 1968, and since then it has become one of the finest all-round recreation lakes in the western half of Texas. Seventy miles in length, this huge reservoir is an outdoor-lover's

Home Away from Home.
Houseboating is a popular sport on Amistad. Boat rentals of all kinds are available at the lake's marinas.

paradise. There's no closed season on fishing, for example, and the lake contains healthy populations of everything from bass to sunfish. Four large park-owned campgrounds and a number of smaller ones are scattered around Amistad, and a dozen private RV parks lie just outside the park boundary on US 90. Boat-launching ramps are numerous and there are two marinas that supply visitors with gas, sundries, fishing tackle, and boat rentals.

Located just a few miles west of Del Rio, Amistad is a true desert lake, today backed up into the deep, barren canyons of the Devils River, the Pecos, and of course the Rio Grande. Not many roads reach the lakeshore except at the southeast end near Amistad Dam, and I found that one of the best ways to explore this massive reservoir is by boat.

I spent my first night on the lake at Spur 406 Campground, a Lilliputian, no-hookups site snuggled into the tamarisk and scrub juniper on the northern shore of the Devils River arm. There I met retired plumbing contractor Jake Burrows and his wife, Amanda, both Minnesota natives who spend their winters at Amistad in a small but well-kept fifth-wheeler.

Catfish for Dinner.
A large Amistad Lake catfish, filleted and fried in corn meal, will make a fine meal for this angler and his family.

At Jake's invitation I accompanied the couple next morning on their daily catfishing trip. By 6 A.M. we were ten miles from the campground, perched on the wooden seats of the Burrows's sixteen-foot-long aluminum outboard, lines out and hooks baited.

"I really can't think of a more pleasant way to spend my retirement," Jake told me as we drifted through a gorgeous West Texas sunrise. "We fish for walleye all summer in Ely, then pack up and head for Texas in October, just about the time the fish start biting. The weather here is great, and the cost of living is so low that I don't have to worry about taking another job. Basically we live on fresh fish and love; that's plenty for anyone."

In between hooking and hauling the sizable yellow catfish that nibbled our bait every few minutes, we spotted all sorts of wildlife on the lakeshore—egret and heron along the bank, duck and geese in the backwaters, quail, dove, and hawk in the surrounding hills. At one point we watched a coyote feed on a too-slow jackrabbit he had captured no more than twenty yards from the boat, and at the mouth of a small canyon I held my breath as a pair of sleek white-tailed does slipped cautiously down to the water to drink. By noon, a dozen large catfish were flopping around in the bottom of the boat, and we headed toward home and shade before the sun became too hot to tolerate. It was one of the most enjoyable mornings I have ever spent.

In the two days that followed I discovered that the most suitable camping areas for RVs at Amistad are at Governor's Landing, Spur 454 Campground, Old 277 South Campground, and Old 277 North Campground, all on the southeastern end of the lake. There are a number of others but

Boater's Paradise.
Quiet coves like this one make Amistad Lake an angling and boating paradise. Located just a few miles west of Del Rio, the reservoir collects water from the Pecos, Rio Grande, and Devils rivers.

most (with the exception of Spur 406 Campground) are either too small for larger vehicles, or their access roads are too rough to negotiate. I spent my final night at a manicured space in Holiday Camp, a private campground on US 90 about a mile from the main Amistad marina. There are about a hundred such sites here and the place comes complete with swimming pool, cable TV hookups, and plenty of quiet.

Del Rio

With my rig's freezer compartment full of catfish fillets, I made the short drive into Del Rio early the next morning. Known as the "Queen City of the Rio Grande," this small desert community isn't particularly attractive from a scenic point of view, but if you happen to like old buildings, it's a place you shouldn't pass by.

First on my list of things to do was take a walking tour of Del Rio's old historic district, most of it located in the downtown area along Griner, Losoya, South Main, and Greenwood streets. Many of the homes here were built in the late nineteenth century, when, because of a newly arrived railroad connecting Del Rio with New Orleans and San Francisco, the town was in full boom. Some of the houses I recommend seeing are the Dardy-Borroum home at 703 Losoya, the Chris Qualia home at 901 South Main, the Tagliabue home at 609 Pecan, and the Taylor-Rivers house at 100 Hudson Drive. Other interesting buildings in the same area you might want to visit are the Old Sacred Heart Church, the town's historic jail, and Val Verde County Courthouse. A walking-driving tour map of Del Rio is available at the chamber of commerce office or at any Texas Tourist Bureau location.

The city also boasts an excellent museum housed in the old Perry store at 1308 South Main Street. Most exhibits in the Whitehead Memorial Museum depict life in the boom-town days of Del Rio and in the frontier west in general (Judge Roy Bean's grave is also located here). And another place I enjoyed was the Val Verde Winery, established in 1883 by Italian immigrants and thought to be the oldest bonded wine-making institution in Texas. The winery's regular business hours are 9 A.M. to 5 P.M. every day except Sunday.

Ciudad Acuna

From Del Rio you can follow Las Vacas Street (SR 239) south four miles to the Rio Grande, cross the U.S.–Mexican border, and visit the small Mexican community of Ciudad Acuna. Small shops and boutiques offering handmade arts and crafts from all over Mexico are abundant in the downtown area, and if you like "south-of-the-border" cuisine there are some excellent restaurants here. Leave your rig at the border and walk over if you want, but if you decide to drive, have your vehicle title (or letter from your bank giving permission to take your RV into Mexico) in possession. You'll also need short-term Mexican insurance, available from travel agencies on both sides of the river. Mexican law states that Americans cannot drive a vehicle of any kind in Mexico unless it is covered by Mexican insurance.

Memories from the West Texas Bush

Once I had completed my tour of historic Del Rio and had contributed my share to the local economy in Ciudad Acuna, I turned south on US 277 and pointed the nose of my rig toward Eagle Pass, fifty-six miles away.

South of Del Rio, US 277 is wide, well-kept, and extremely scenic as it runs adjacent to the border along the Rio Grande, and though motorists can't really notice much from the road, animal life in the thick bush is profuse. Besides the larger critters such as deer, bobcats, coyotes, and javelina, every rock, tree, and stump has its little family of lizards, centipedes, mice, rats, spiders, or the large, black, crablike vinegarroons, also known as "whip scorpions." Naturally there are snakes as well, including the diamondback rattler.

Several years ago, with permission from a local rancher, I spent a few days backpacking in the mesquite bush south of Del Rio to see what mischief I could get into. Without much planning (which is the way I like to hike), I left my small RV at the rancher's house, and set off across the

Diamonds Aren't a Hiker's Best Friend.
This Texas diamondback rattlesnake, coiled and ready to strike, is not a pleasant sight to anyone except a herpetologist.

Border Country Sundown.
There are few prettier sights than a hazy west Texas sun settling into the horizon, such as this one in the bush country east of Del Rio.

country in a wide circle that would hopefully bring me back to my starting point in three to four days.

The first two days went pretty much as expected. Early afternoon of the third day, however, found me perched on the lip of a low ridge, thoroughly lost. The bush had become so thick in some places that to move forward I had to backtrack, looking for another route. Somehow I had tracked back once too often and become totally turned around. Meriwether Lewis I'm not.

Disgusted but reasonably sure I could locate the ranch house at dawn, I camped beneath a large mesquite tree, carefully explored my ridge, cooked supper, and observed the West Texas sunset in all its primordial splendor. Then, just before full dark, as I was about to throw my sleeping bag on the ground near the fire, I glimpsed a spot of unnatural color beneath a nearby bush. The "spot" was a four-foot-long diamondback rattlesnake that had no doubt stumbled into my camp while hunting. He licked his lips as I approached, stared at my leg, and flicked his tongue.

Deer, coyotes, javelina, skunks, and badgers—all of which I had observed during the past three days—I didn't mind. I am not, however, overly fond of rattlesnakes. Nasty little creatures in my opinion, they bite when you aren't looking. I don't kill them unless they create a hazard though, and this one wasn't—at least not yet. What he was, was stubborn, refusing to go about his business even when I clobbered him with a nickle-sized stone. He poked his tongue at my effort. I rattled the bush, careful to keep out of range. He rattled his tail in answer.

I'll share the desert with rattlers if they keep their distance, but under no circumstance will I allow one to sleep with me. This fellow seemed to

Gather Ye Rosebuds.
A young girl gathers wildflowers near Eagle Pass.

Bountiful Basket.
Fresh fruits and vegetables are but a few of the items available at Speedy's Swap Mart in Seco Mines.

have little fear and would no doubt have crawled into my sleeping bag to stay warm in the evening chill. Since it was almost dark and I didn't want a bed partner, he would have to depart. I tried another rock and he answered with a long, malevolent buzz.

The nearest large boulder was a jagged chunk of flint, one foot square and two inches thick. I picked it up, took careful aim, then in a fit of compassion changed my mind. Cutting a dried mesquite branch from my camp tree, I carefully slid it beneath the snake and half carried, half dragged the critter to a gully 100 yards away. The ungrateful wretch dropped in a heap, coiled, poked his tongue again, and finally slithered off into the grass. How close he came to becoming a hat band, he would never know.

Eagle Pass

I stopped for lunch at Mary's Cafe in the small farm town of Quemado, then continued along US 277 to the border city of Eagle Pass. Originally settled during the Mexican War, this scruffy little town doesn't have many obvious attractions for RVers, but if you have the time and inclination, there are a couple of treasures here that will surprise you.

One is old Fort Duncan, established in 1849, and today located between Bliss and Adams streets downtown. The fort was deactivated in 1916, but several of the old buildings have been restored, and there's a small museum on the grounds displaying frontier artifacts. The museum is open by appointment only; if you're interested, contact the curator at (512) 775-2241.

Another attraction is Piedras Negras, the small sister city of Eagle Pass, located just across the Rio Grande. The downtown area of this community of 33,000 is a shopper's delight, brimming with hole-in-the-wall stores, galleries, and small markets. To get there turn west on US 57 and follow it across the International Bridge. (Once again, don't forget to buy Mexican insurance first, and don't cross the border without a vehicle title or "letter of removal" from your bank.)

Finally, in the Eagle Pass suburb of Seco Mines, you will find Speedy's Swap Mart, open only on Saturday. Beyond a doubt the most extensive collection of previously owned implements of our culture (junk) in all of West Texas, Speedy's is well worth an hour of your time. Located beneath a grove of large shade trees on the edge of town, the flea market's 200 or so stalls offer sightseers everything from used coat hangers to handmade cowboy boots, all naturally at cut-rate prices. There's a wide, grassy embankment adjacent to US 277 were you can park and have plenty of room to maneuver. The market is open every Saturday throughout the year.

Eagle Pass has no RV facilities but if you plan to stay more than one day, Bowman Village RV Park is about fifteen miles west of town on US 277. I spent the night here and was pleasantly surprised to find this isolated camp both charming and comfortable. Bowman's is located on the south side of the highway near Quemado. (It provides all hookups.)

Implements of Our Culture.
Whatever you want in the way of other people's treasures you'll find at Speedy's Swap Mart. One of the largest flea markets in Texas, the place is a paradise for bargain shoppers.

Along the Cowboy Trail

Though even most Texans don't know it, the 125-mile drive between Eagle Pass and Laredo via US 277 and US 83 bisects a segment of American history that was as important to the border country as the Mexican War. It was here, in the mid-1800s, among the thorny mesquite forests and vast fields of cacti that the culture of the American cowboy was born.

Sometime in the 1700s, probably in the early part of the century, large numbers of wild-eyed and ornery longhorn cattle began to drift north across the Rio Grande from ranches in northern Mexico. With virtually no natural predators, the cattle multiplied rapidly in the thick bush northwest of Laredo. Within a few short decades, historians tell us, they numbered in the hundreds of thousands. Responding to a clamor from beef-hungry America, Texans on horseback began to round up the longhorns, and by 1875 virtually thousands had been removed from the bush and driven to railheads in Missouri and Kansas over the thousand-mile-long Sedalia and Chisholm trails.

Contrary to what most of us believe, the cowboy's life was hardly romantic. The task of separating the cattle from their traditional thorny home, for instance, was not the easiest chore on earth. Not only was the mesquite so thick in places it could not be breached by a man on horseback, but the cattle themselves were not overly eager to leave. More than one nineteenth-century drover was buried on the desert after being stomped into mush by the stubborn, oversized longhorns.

If the cows were mean, however, cowboys were meaner—hard-riding, dust-breathing brawlers who ate beans and dried beef for weeks on end and were paid $40 a month (no raises) for their trouble. A cowboy's only

Up in Flames!
Burning weeds is a fact of farm and
ranch life in the border country of
Texas. Using a machine instead of
matches is a quick solution to an
old problem.

job was to play nursemaid. His only possessions were a saddle, the clothes
on his back, and a heavy, well-oiled revolver that was accurate only if the
target was unmoving and less than five yards away.

Mainly because of barbed wire and a wider network of railroads (that
came to the cattle), the heyday of the cowboy ended about 1900. Longhorns too, in heavy competition with meat-rich breeds like Herefords,
almost disappeared, but are now beginning to reappear on some of the
larger Texas ranches. You'll probably see several herds of these huge
animals grazing alongside the highway between Eagle Pass and Laredo. If
you stop to take a picture, I recommend keeping a fence between you and
your subject. Just because a few centuries have passed does not mean that
the longhorn's nature has become less churlish.

Laredo

Founded in 1755 by a captain in the Spanish colonial army, Laredo did not
join the Union until 1846 when General Zach Taylor and a group of Texas
Rangers took the local garrison away from the Mexican army. Two years
later, when the treaty of Guadalupe Hidalgo was signed and the Rio
Grande was declared the official boundary between Mexico and the
United States, Laredo split in half, both politically and physically. Many
residents stayed where they were and accepted American rule, but others,
those who wished to remain loyal to Mexico, moved to a new location
across the river and founded the Mexican town of Nuevo Laredo.

You may want to pass by these two border cities, especially if you
aren't fond of traffic. Because of narrow streets, heavy auto congestion,

and lack of RV facilities, the downtown areas are certainly not a motorhome or travel-trailer paradise. Yet these two small communities, one on each side of the river and both steeped lovingly in fiery Latin influence, offer a fresh, lively, fiestalike atmosphere to visitors and residents alike. If you decide to stay for a few days, I can almost promise that you won't regret the decision.

RVing in Laredo

It's hard to believe that Laredo, a city of 100,000, has not a single RV park of its own. There are, however, a couple of suitable alternatives. One is to stay free at the Texas Tourist Bureau on I-35 a few miles north of town. Hookups aren't available, but the parking lot here is large, paved, and surrounded by a pleasant botanical garden. If your rig is not self-contained, there are restrooms inside the building. A second alternative is to park at Lake Casa Blanca, a small lakeshore picnic and recreation area located on Laredo's eastern side three miles from the I-35–US 59 junction. Again, you won't have hookups, but the park is free, usually quiet, and each site is equipped with picnic tables and fire grills.

I camped out on the Texas Tourist Bureau parking lot, primarily because of its access to the downtown area. By accident I ran into Mike Conchas, director of the city's convention and visitor's bureau, and he recommended against driving my rig into the city. Traffic at any time of the day is heavy, Mike told me, and downtown Laredo is a spiderweb of narrow streets. Since I wasn't pulling a tag-along, he suggested I call a cab or join a city tour sponsored by the Webb County Heritage Foundation.

"Remember," he said apologetically, "Laredo was originally meant for oxen carts and horses, not RVs."

The Historic District

Following Mike's advice, I took a taxi into Laredo (about $8). My first stop was the colorful historic district, still the city's hub as it was 200 years ago and a wonderful place to explore for a few hours. If you have time for nothing else, be sure to visit the famous San Augustin Church, built in 1872, and old Fort McIntosh, established in 1848 to guard Laredo against Indian attack.

There are two fine museums here, both of them open every day. The Capitol of the Republic of the Rio Grande Museum on Zaragoza Street near San Augustin Plaza has an excellent collection of weapons, saddles, household goods, and other artifacts used by early residents of the city. A similar collection can be found in the Nuevo Santander Museum in Fort McIntosh. Probably the most unusual exhibit at Nuevo Santander is a traditional *jacal*—a primitive sandstone-and-cane hut in which Mexican peasants lived well into the twentieth century.

If you like to shop, stroll through the open-air bazaar, El Mercado, in Old City Hall Square. Vendors with small carts will try to sell you everything from popcorn to silver jewelry. For a quick getaway, a dime will get

Antique Church.
Laredo's ancient San Augustin Church, built in 1872, attracts many visitors to the city.

Outdoor Market.
Fruit and vegetable vendors offer their wares to passersby in a Nuevo Laredo street market. This south-of-the-border city is a bit shabby, but it is a shopper's paradise nonetheless.

you a ride on the Laredo trolley. This quaint passenger train operates throughout the day in the historic district and stops at most of the area's major attractions.

Nuevo Laredo

Laredo's sister city, Nuevo Laredo, is located just across the Rio Grande on the Mexican side of the border. Again, Mike Conchas recommended that I not attempt to drive, and after my visit there I have to agree. Traffic congestion is so bad that it often takes half an hour just to go a few blocks. The quickest way to reach Nuevo Laredo from the historic district is to take a cab. Ask to be dropped at the Convent Avenue Bridge, then walk across. The cost to enter Mexico at this writing was fifteen cents.

City streets here are lined with hundreds of tiny shops, but for better quality—especially in artwork, jewelry, and fine clothing—I suggest Marti's, a get-it-all-here complex on Calle Victoria (Victoria Street). For a more casual kind of shopping, visit Nuevo Laredo's central market a block south, where vendors sell clothing and handicrafts from open-air stalls. If you don't like the prices here remember that Mexican vendors expect Americans to haggle and would probably be surprised and insulted if they didn't. There is one other interesting activity in Nuevo Laredo you might enjoy. Greyhound races are held Wednesday through Sunday evening at Nuevo Laredo Downs, six miles south of the city. To get there catch the El Metro shuttle bus from Laredo's Riverside Mall or the Mall Del Norte. The bus ride costs $6 round trip and can be arranged by calling the track's travel service at (512) 726-0540.

POINTS OF INTEREST: Texas Tour 2

West Texas

0   20MI

0   50KM

ACCESS: From Langtry, take *US 90* east to *US 277*; follow *US 277* southeast to *US 83*; stay on *US 83* to Laredo.

INFORMATION: *Judge Roy Bean Visitor Center,* PO Box 160, Langtry, TX 78871, (915) 292-3340; *Seminole Canyon State Historical Park,* PO Box 820, Comstock, TX 78837, (915) 292-4464; *Amistad National Recreation Area,* Star Route #2, Box 5-P, Highway 90 West, Del Rio, TX 78840, (512) 775-6491; *Del Rio Chamber of Commerce,* 1915 Avenue F, Del Rio, TX 78840, (512) 775-3551; *Eagle Pass Chamber of Commerce,* PO Box 1188, Eagle Pass, TX 78852, (512) 773-3224; *Laredo Chamber of Commerce,* PO Box 790, Laredo, TX 78042, (512) 722-9895.

ANNUAL EVENTS:

Del Rio: *Fiesta de Amistad* (beauty pagent, parades, fireworks, dances), October.

Eagle Pass: *George Washington International Fiesta* (Latin-accented balls, pageantry, parades), March; *Old Men's Roping* (old-timer's cowboy events), October.

Laredo: *Washington Birthday Celebration* (dances, bullfights, fireworks), February; *Border Olympics* (track and field events); *International Fair & Exposition* (exhibitions, fairs, rodeos, horse shows), March.

MUSEUMS & GALLERIES:

Langtry: *Judge Roy Bean Visitor Center,* open 8 A.M.–5 P.M. year-round, frontier artifacts.

Del Rio: *Whitehead Memorial Museum,* 1308 Main Street, open Tuesday through Saturday 9 A.M.–4:30 P.M., admission.

Laredo: *Capitol of the Republic of the Rio Grande Museum,* 1000 Zaragoza Street, open 10 A.M. to 5 P.M. Tuesday through Sunday, frontier artifacts; *Nuevo Santander Museum,* Washington Street and the Rio Grande, open 9 A.M.–4 P.M. Monday through Friday, old documents, photos, and buildings; *Hinojosa Art Gallery,* Clark Street, watercolors, sculpture.

RESTAURANTS:

Del Rio: *El Sombrero,* 2116 Ave. F, Mexican food; *Wrights Steak House,* Hwy 90 W., home cooking.

Ciudad Acuna: *Crosby's,* Hidalgo y Matamoros streets, Mexican food, seafood.

Eagle Pass: *Charcoal Grill,* Del Rio Highway N., American/Mexican food.

Laredo: *Unicorn Restaurant,* San Bernardo Street, steaks, seafood; *Cotulla's Pit Bar-B-Que,* McPherson St., Mexican food, Texas barbecue.

Nuevo Laredo: *La Noria,* five blocks south of Convent Ave. Bridge on Acampo Ave., Mexican food, seafood.

South Texas

They call this place where the Swift River of the North comes rolling onto the unbelievably green plains, the Valley. It doesn't seem to have any other name. To Texans there can be only one Valley, just as there can be only one Paradise—or one Texas. And this is it.

Robert J. Casey,
The Texas Border

When I'm traveling, everyday about 4 P.M. I start thinking about my own little piece of ground. It can be a space in an RV park or state campground, alongside the highway, even in the middle of a wheat field if nothing else is available. It's *my* piece of ground, though, *my* space, a private niche where I can button up the blinds, turn on the air conditioner, light up the radio or TV, plop a meal in the oven, fix a tall, cool drink, and forget those white lines on the black asphalt that have been slipping by all day.

It was that time of afternoon—just west of the town of Mission in the South Texas tropics—when I saw the herd of elephants. A small herd to be sure, but elephants nonetheless, staked on short tethers within a few yards of US 83, causing a traffic problem as they munched slowly but strategically on a large mound of hay. Two hundred feet off the highway a huge, billowing, colorful circus tent had been erected, but the animals themselves were untended and had attracted a crowd. Thirty or so people, most of them bright-eyed Hispanic children, had gathered in a semi-circle and were watching in awe as the great grey beasts fanned the air with their trunks, spewing clouds of half-eaten hay in the process.

I was tired, hungry, and far from being settled for the night, but I couldn't help myself. I pulled over, walked back up the highway, and joined the crowd of grinning children and sun-wizened old folks who were observing the spectacle with every ounce of concentration they could muster. As I mentioned earlier, one never knows what will turn up on a Texas highway, and certainly this was one of those "whats." The sprawling Lower Rio Grande Valley up ahead—better known to local RVers as the Texas Tropical Trail—could wait a few minutes. It was time to unwind, make like a kid, throw a few peanuts, and poke fun at the pachyderms. Some things are just too good to miss.

Tour 3 365 miles

MISSION • BENTSEN RIO GRANDE STATE PARK • BROWNSVILLE • SOUTH PADRE ISLAND • LAGUNA ATASCOSA NATIONAL WILDLIFE REFUGE • PORT ISABEL • PORT MANSFIELD • KINGSVILLE • ARANSAS PASS • PORT ARANSAS • ROCKPORT • ARANSAS NATIONAL WILDLIFE REFUGE

Mission

Mission, Texas, advertises itself as the home of the famous Texas Ruby Red grapefruit; indeed, it is the commercial hub for the vast crop of citrus fruit grown each year in the surrounding area. Here too occurs America's only all-poinsettia flower show, which employs the unusual theme each December of "Tropical Christmas." The town itself is attractive and picturesque, nestled down among the citrus groves and prolific farmlands at the western edge of the Lower Rio Grande Valley. RVers love the quiet neighborhoods, dry, mild climate, and rural atmosphere here, and because of that love, Mission abounds with RV parks. Ten thousand spaces exist presently within a five-mile radius of town, and more are being constructed every day.

Evening on the Guadalupe.
A catfisherman glides toward his camp on the Guadalupe River near Aransas National Wildlife Refuge. His flat-bottomed "John boat" is standard equipment for south Texas anglers.

The Texas state highway system encompasses 74,019 miles of designated highways, of which 41,803 miles (all paved) are farm, ranch, and recreational roads (better known as "backroads"). On this system are more than a million signs and markers, and at least 1,000 roadside turnouts, rest areas, picnic areas, and scenic overlooks.

Four miles west of Mission, I exited US 83 and turned south onto FM 374, and after another three miles turned right again onto FM 2062. I'd been told by another RVer that some of Mission's most pleasant RV campgrounds could be found on FM 2062, and sure enough there lay an entire row of parks, all of them as picture-perfect as an ad out of *Better Homes & Gardens.* I chose the Kountry Korral because of its wide access road, signed up with campground host Ken Mosely, and was promptly shown to a quiet grassy space without neighbors. Mosely did most of the hookup work, then kindly invited me to wash off my coating of half-chewed elephant fodder in the park's swirling Jacuzzi.

The next morning I drove into Mission for a tour of the famous South Texas Wildlife Museum and Gallery, featuring among other exhibits a natural-history display of mounted wild animals found in the area. I also visited Capilla de la Lomita (Chapel of the Little Hill), an ancient adobe rest station for priests and other travelers who headed north from Brownsville in the mid-1800s. This interesting structure, built by the Oblate Fathers, still exhibits the original brick floors, beehive-shaped bread oven, and original water well. Adjacent to the chapel is a seven-acre park with picnic facilities. La Lomita is located three miles south of town on FM 1016.

Bentsen Rio Grande State Park

After my tour of Mission, I drove to Bentsen Rio Grande State Park, lying along the Rio Grande at the south end of FM 2062 (about a mile south of the Kountry Korral RV Park), where I spent the night.

If you're looking for rustic and isolated camping in the Mission area, this 600-acre, wildlife-filled riverside preserve simply cannot be bested. The park's interior is junglelike in appearance, heavily wooded with cedar elm, hackberry, sweet acacia, coyotillo, and a hundred other species of tree, shrub, and bush. Nearly 80 RV sites, many of them with hookups, are scattered beneath this thick, green canopy; in addition, the park provides showers, restrooms, a small fishing lake with boat ramp, even playgrounds for the children. More than 200 species of birds reside here, among them such rarities as Audubon's oriole and the red-eye cowbird. Nature trails are plentiful, and bicyclers will be pleasantly surprised to find that all interior roads are paved.

My only visitors that night were a pair of local raccoons who seemed interested in devouring my sewer pipe. I helped them back into the woods with a few well-directed pebbles, slept like a baby in the park's overwhelming nighttime silence, and just after dawn returned to US 83 and headed southeast for Brownsville.

Brownsville

Established in 1846, Brownsville is now the Lower Rio Grande Valley's largest (population 95,000) city. The suburbs, scattered among the palm trees and quiet canal-like *resacas,* are quite attractive, but the downtown

Motionless Beauty.
A pink flamingo in the Gladys Porter Zoo might stand in the same unmoving position throughout the entire day.

Peaceful Panorama.
Sunset in Bentsen Rio Grande State Park
is the prettiest time of day.

area with its narrow streets and heavy traffic is not a place I'd visit more than necessary.

The city does contain several points of interest that you might want to see, however. One of my favorites is the Gladys Porter Zoo, an elaborate zoological park in which most of the animals reside on small islands or in other totally natural settings. Another is the Brownsville Historical Museum, featuring photo exhibits and other displays and artifacts portraying the city's early years. If you don't mind putting up with traffic, pop over to the shopping malls of Matamoros, Mexico, just across the Rio Grande (access is via the Gateway Bridge at the end of East 14th Street). And for a pleasant day trip, drive out to Brazos Island State Park, twenty-two miles east on SR 4. The park is not actually an island, but a small spit of land in the Gulf Of Mexico known as Boca Chica (little mouth). The beach here is undeveloped and has no facilities, but swimming and fishing are superb.

If you decide to stay in Brownsville for a few days, there are plenty of RV parks in town from which to choose. Two that I can recommend personally are Crooked Tree Campland at the junction of US 83 and

Varied Wares.
A pottery vendor in Matamoros, Mexico, offers fine Mexican pottery to American tourists. This particular style was originally made by Zapotec Indians hundreds of years ago.

FM 802, and River Bend Resort, three miles west of town on US 281. One last suggestion, especially if you like to fish: Many of the small bodies of water (*resacas*) in Brownsville contain healthy populations of large crappie. Find yourself a bucket of minnows, make sure you're fishing on public land, and you can generally take home enough of these tasty, wide-bodied panfish in one sitting to feed a small army.

The Best Little Island in Texas

The most prominent sound on South Padre Island is the overpowering roar of the surf. Like thunder before a desert storm, it rolls dramatically across the landscape, bellowing displeasure at being restrained by the hard-packed sand of the beach. Even when the tide is out and the north wind sleeps, the surf god roars belligerence; only those who truly trust in the providence of the sea can listen without knowing fear.

I scribbled those words in my journal one mellow December evening a few years ago, at the front end of my first RV vacation on South Padre Island. Since then, although I've returned a number of times, the feeling of trifling unimportance I experienced during that initial visit hasn't changed. The island forever belongs to the sea, and no matter where you are or how long you stay, it won't easily let you forget.

Located in the Gulf of Mexico just eighteen miles east of Brownsville (at the end of SR 100), and proudly nicknamed "the best little island in Texas" by local residents, this skinny, thirty-four-mile-long, mile-wide barrier island is an RVer's paradise. There are three spacious camping parks on South Padre—all of them modest in cost—and RV camping is

Up and Up.
The town of South Padre, once little more than a few huts and a bar, is now a popular tourist resort, complete with high-rise condos and hotels. Nonetheless, at the north village limits, civilization ceases and nothing but a sandy wilderness awaits.

also allowed on the public beach. Winter weather is mild, and such outdoor pursuits as fishing, sailing, diving, and beachcombing are readily available. Moreover, the island is one of those atypical vacation areas where visitors are treated with respect and friendliness by the locals. Personally, I've never quite become used to the genuine hospitality shown to travelers by the island folk. I felt as though I had lived there all of my life.

Most long-time visitors to South Padre Island say that in the three decades since this narrow strip of sand and sawgrass was first linked to Port Isabel and the mainland by bridge, not much has changed but the south-end skyline.

"Hotels and condos started popping up in the village a few years ago," one retired army officer told me, "but two minutes out of town and you're in the boonies. Fishing is still the best on the Texas coast, bird watching is phenomenal, and the beachcombing is absolutely superb. I don't even notice the new construction anymore."

The island is seemingly one of those exceptional places that has accommodated both recreational interests and suburban expansion without sacrificing its fragile oceanside hinterland. Permanent human habitation and all RV and camping parks, for instance, are restricted to South Padre Village, a small resort community on the southernmost tip. But at the north village limits, civilization ceases abruptly, and for a distance of nearly thirty miles there is nothing but shell-encrusted beach, sea birds, and a sandy wilderness of wind-sculpted dunes and waving sawgrass. The first eleven miles of the island are bisected by a paved highway (PR 100), but past that all travel is on hard-packed sand along the gulf.

Gold on the Beach

Historians say that during the War of 1812, pirate Jean Lafitte supposedly buried half a million dollars in pilfered gold bullion on the gulfside beach of South Padre, but never returned to claim his hoard. Another version of the story claims that indeed, he did return, but couldn't find where *X* marked the spot because of a recent terrain-changing storm.

Whether either tale is true, only Lafitte knows for sure (and he isn't telling), but today, though gold coins occasionally wash up on the beach after a storm, the island has plenty of other treasures that are easier to find. After a high tide, for example, South Padre's beaches are generally littered with the flotsam of the sea. Shells by the thousands cover the sand, as do rarer samples of man's and nature's handiwork: glass fishing floats, collectible bottles, and nightmarish creatures from the ocean's depths. In addition to being a beachcomber's nirvana, the northern area of South Padre is one of the finest bird-watching sanctuaries in Texas. More than 300 different species have been observed in the past few years, from the rare peregrine falcon and roseate spoonbill to more common inhabitants such as brown pelicans, curlews, and skimmers.

It is the ancient and honorable sport of fishing, though, that attracts more RVers to the island than anything else. From November through March, when huge schools of Gulf of Mexico gamefish migrate inshore to breed, angling fever here reaches epidemic proportions. Surfcasters equipped with long, whiplike rods and heavy reels catch pompano, whiting, black drum, and redfish off the beach, while across the island in Laguna Madre Bay, anglers using lighter tackle land speckled trout, flounder, and smaller drum and redfish. The most interesting thing about fishing here is that you never know *what* you'll catch. It could be a two-pound trout or a thirty-pound "bull" redfish, but it will always be a surprise.

Other Island Delights

The active South Padre Island Tourist Bureau claims "something for everyone," and they are probably right. In the small community of South Padre Village, for instance, a hodgepodge of hotels, gourmet restaurants, discos, rental shops, grocery stores, and service stations line the four-and-a-half-mile-long Padre Boulevard. Here you can buy or rent everything from a lobster dinner to a wind-surfing board. For kids there are easily operated go-carts, and a fishing pier. One of the island's most popular

Reds for the Pot.
Redfish is one of the most popular gamefish on South Padre Island, as well as one of the best eating gamefish in North America. The recent craze for blackened redfish, however, is endangering this species.

family adventures is a cruise on Laguna Madre Bay aboard the *Isabella Queen,* an authentic "Old South" paddle-wheeler tour boat, moored at a downtown dock.

Two of the three RV parks on the island are owned and operated by the Cameron County Parks system, while the other—Fisherman's Wharf—is managed privately. A total of 414 spaces are available, all of them with full RV hookups. The three camping areas are located on the southern end of South Padre; to get there turn right just off the causeway onto Padre Boulevard. Camping on either Laguna Madre or gulfside beaches is "pick-your-own-spot" and costs nothing. Be sure, however, to choose a campsite that is well above the high-tide line, for obvious reasons.

Side Trip to Laguna Atascosa

If you're interested in wildlife photography—mainly of birds—Laguna Atascosa National Wildlife Refuge eighteen miles north of Port Isabel is a must. From the first of November through late March, millions of ducks, geese, cranes, and shorebirds call this 45,000-acre refuge home. Park headquarters is located just off the main highway and is well marked. There is one main tour route that winds through the thick brush and salt marsh along the coast and is completely suitable for RVs. Pick up a bird list at the visitor center; the refuge is open during daylight hours every day except federal holidays.

Port Isabel—Confederate Air Force

I spent four days on South Padre, toured the shrimp boats and famous old lighthouse at Port Isabel (on the mainland just over the causeway from the island), then returned to US 77 and headed north toward the city of Harlingen. I might mention that Port Isabel is also a popular RVer's town, but beach access here is limited. If you want to fill your larder with shrimp or other seafood, though, this is the place. Any fish or bait shop along the main street will offer a wide selection of whatever *marisco* happens to be in season.

Just north of Harlingen, I turned right onto FM 508, drove east for three miles, then turned right again onto FM 507, heading for the famed Confederate Air Force Flying Museum at the Harlingen airport. Dedicated to acquisition, restoration, and preservation (in flying condition) of vintage military aircraft, the museum is an entertaining place to spend a morning. The thirty or so aircraft parked on the tarmac here date from 1939 to 1945 and include such famous ships of war as the P-40 *Warhawk,* P-38 *Lightning,* P-47 *Thunderbolt,* British *Spitfire,* and German *Messerschmitt.* All are operational or in the process of becoming so.

I don't fly personally but I've always been a nut for airplanes, and in my opinion this is one of the most enjoyable attractions of the Lower Rio Grande Valley. Visitors, of course, are welcome to wander among the planes and to tour the really excellent weapons museum adjacent to the tarmac. The complex is open Monday through Saturday from 9 A.M. till

Guess Who's Coming to Dinner.
A gleaming white egret patiently waits for a school of minnows to swim by so he can pounce.

Light of Life.
The old lighthouse at Port Isabel, just across the bay from South Padre Island, has probably kept more than its share of ships off the beach. The structure is open for public inspection every day of the year.

Shrimp Boats Are a'Comin'.
The Port Isabel shrimp fleet is one of the largest in the nation, furnishing fresh seafood, not only for the south Texas region, but for much of the United States as well.

5 P.M., and on Sundays and holidays from 1 P.M. till 6 P.M. If you happen to visit in October, don't miss the fabulous "Airsho" during which the planes duel and dogfight in the skies above the airport.

Port Mansfield

The flat, open farm country along US 77 north of Harlingen is relatively boring to motorists, but the highway is dotted with colorful fruit stands offering locally grown citrus and fresh vegetables. Most of the stands are open throughout the year and are as inexpensive as you might expect.

Twenty-three miles north of Harlingen, my fifty-pound sack of Texas Ruby Red grapefruit and I left US 77 and turned east onto SR 186, a straight-as-an-arrow "farm access" road leading to the small coastal village of Port Mansfield. After ten or twelve miles I began to see herds of huge African and Asian antelope grazing near the highway. I discovered later that the animals are part of a large ranch in the area and are raised specifically for the purpose of sport hunting by paying customers. Local farmers, I was told, used to seeing cattle or jackrabbits along the road, get a far bigger kick out of simply watching the graceful creatures than they ever would by shooting them.

Port Mansfield, with a population of only about 700, is neither a resort town nor a fishing village—at least in the traditional sense. It is instead a small, attractive coastal community on Laguna Madre Bay that is searching, not too frantically, for an identity in the heavily tourist-oriented atmosphere of South Texas. The town did not exist at all, in fact, until 1948 when the good folks of Willacy Country—using their own financing and resources—built the place up out of a salt marsh. Today its principal claims to fame are the small shrimp fleet based here and an obscure rating as one of the ten best saltwater fishing spots in America.

Port Mansfield boasts two RV parks, the R & R Campground on the western edge of town and the Bayview RV Park on Bayview Drive. The remainder of the community consists of a few beach houses, an apartment complex, a small harbor area with adjacent bait-and-tackle shop, and a grocery store or two. Noticeably missing are the high-rise hotels and condos and busy main thoroughfares so common in closer-to-civilization resort areas of the same size.

I chose the R & R Campground simply because it was less busy than the other. I paid my modest fee and was pointed to a level space in the center of what seemed to be an unused cow pasture. Moments after I pulled through, I was cornered by two men named Clyde and Mike, dressed in shorts and fishing vests, who proceeded to tell me about the superb red fishing, speckled trout fishing, and crabbing in Port Mansfield. Part of the conversation went something like this:

"Dang good fishin' here," said Clyde.

"Ain't really bad," Mike said, "'specially if you know what you're doin'."

"Must not be very good for you then," Clyde commented, poking my ribs with his elbow. "No how, no way, do you know what you're doin'."

"Least I know which end of a boat goes forward and which end goes back," Mike answered, winking.

"Then why you always gettin' that thing you call a boat hung up on a sandbar?" countered Clyde, pointing to what I assumed was Mike's sixteen-foot-long aluminum skiff, sitting alongside his RV.

In the following five minutes, Clyde got pinched on the arm by a blue crab—one he had picked out of a bucket to show me—and Mike's fishing reel developed a tremendous rat's nest as he illustrated the proper way to cast for redfish in the Port Mansfield surf. I learned that the best place in town to buy fresh shrimp was right in the corner of the campground. I was offered the chance to go fishing the following morning (which I accepted). I was also offered the chance to handle a large, angry blue crab with snapping claws (which I declined). My mama didn't raise no fool.

Later that evening I purchased two pounds of large shrimp from a friendly, wizened woman who ran the impromptu corner bait shop, and prepared them using a recipe I once discovered in Louisiana's Cajun country. I dumped the shrimp into a gallon pot of boiling water, added "crab-boil" spices (available in any seacoast grocery), let them cook until pink, then drained off the water and let them cool. After peeling, I fried the shrimp for about thirty seconds in a mixture of hot butter, salt, pepper, and minced garlic. Accompanied by a green salad and buttered bread, fresh or frozen shrimp prepared in this manner will virtually melt in your mouth.

Crab Grab.
A Port Mansfield fisherman shows off the large crab he captured in nearby Laguna Madre Bay. Crab and other shellfish are for sale in several town shops.

Oiling a Squeak.
A cowboy puts a few drops of much-needed oil on the mechanical innards of a ranch windmill. In many areas of south Texas, windmills are still used to pump underground water from wells to above-ground tanks.

Ranch Country

Clyde and I left the park at dawn the next morning, launched his skiff at Port Mansfield's handy boat ramp, and by 9 A.M. we had filled several large buckets with three- to four-pound speckled trout. About noon, I rejoined US 77 and headed north toward Kingsville. Just past the junction, a sign informed me there were no services on the highway for a distance of fifty miles. The sign surprised me until I remembered that this particular section of Texas is encompassed by some of the largest cattle ranches in the world.

The country here is flat, brushy, and covered with grass that is belly-high on a cow. Cattle spreads, such as the Kenedy Ranch, the Yturria Ranch, and of course the famous King Ranch, are almost unbelievable in size and scope, often embracing several hundred thousand acres. Generally, ranch headquarters are small cities unto themselves, each boasting its own power supply, transport system, airstrip, and internal politics. Some even have their own schools, physicians, and dentists.

The biggest and grandest of them all is the legendary King Ranch, established in 1853 and today spread out across more than 800,000 acres of South Texas bush country. Texas longhorns were originally raised by the Kings, but presently the primary beef cow is the Santa Gertrudis—a mix of three-eighths Brahma and five-eighths shorthorn, the first strain of cattle actually developed in the Western Hemisphere. At Kingsville (named, naturally, for the ranch), I visited the John E. Conner Museum to learn a bit about the ranch's history, then drove the twelve-mile-long loop road (SR 141) that bisects part of the property. Casual "drop-ins" to ranch heaquarters aren't really welcome, but you can drive the road anytime you wish, passing feeding pens, quarter horses, and an auction ring on your tour.

Aransas Pass

I bypassed the city of Corpus Christi mainly because traffic in this coastal community of 260,000 is fairly heavy, but there are a number of interesting things to do and see here if you don't mind the congestion. A popular visitor attraction in Corpus, for instance, is the Bayfronts Arts and Science Park, located at the foot of the harbor bridge. With its museums, galleries, parks, and playhouses, Bayfronts is a pleasant place in which to spend a morning. For more information on both the park and city, I suggest a visit to the Corpus Christi Tourist Bureau at 1201 North Shoreline Boulevard.

Just east of Corpus, I turned right on I-37, followed it to Nueces Bay, then left the freeway and turned north on US 181. On the north side of the Corpus Ship Channel and Nueces Bay, I picked up SR 35, the quickest route for RVers to the town of Aransas Pass.

Named for the ship channel between the barrier islands of Mustang and St. Joseph, the small fishing and port town of Aransas Pass offers little to RVers except a place in which to resupply. The shrimp boats moored in Conn Brown Harbor make a nice photograph on a sunny day, but the

Keeping the Country Moving.
An oil refinery in Corpus Christi, although not attractive, provides much-needed jobs for the south Texas coast.

place is a bit rough and I wouldn't visit the harbor region on a Saturday night. I looked for, but could not find, the Seamen's Memorial Tower, dedicated to sailors lost at sea. Tower access is unmarked, and the town's narrow streets are not conducive to backing up or turning around in a thirty-three-foot-long motorhome.

East of Aransas Pass, however, the long, narrow causeway (SR 361) leading to Mustang Island is a camper's paradise. At Morrison Cut, for instance, there's a beautiful little RV park called Fin & Feather on the south side of the highway. It sits at the very edge of Aransas Bay, and guests can actually fish or watch sea birds from their front door if they wish. Lots of free camping can be found here as well, most of it along the bayshore. The sandy access roads off the main highway are a bit rutty, but getting off the pavement isn't a problem if you do it carefully.

Port Aransas

I spent the night alone on a quiet patch of sand near the water, and early next morning drove to the terminus of SR 361 where I caught the car ferry to Port Aransas. These sturdy little craft run twenty-four hours a day

Patience Will Pay Off.
Anglers near Port Aransas wait for a bite in quiet bay waters. In the background, a newly constructed offshore oil rig waits passage to its final resting place in the gulf.

and can take RVs up to fifty-five feet in length. The crossing is free, both going and coming.

Originally founded by an English settler in 1855, Port Aransas encompasses the north end of Mustang Island and is one of the most popular tourist destinations on the Gulf Coast. Like most resort towns, its streets are lined with all sorts of shops, galleries, and restaurants, and even window shoppers can enjoy themselves here. One place you shouldn't bypass if you like vintage buildings is the unrestored Tarpon Inn (where Franklin D. Roosevelt once slept), constructed in 1886. Another is the abundantly stocked viewing aquarium at the University of Texas Marine Science Institute.

Fourteen miles south of town on Park Road 53 there are plenty of campsites with hookups at Mustang Island State Park. Swimming, fishing, and beachcombing at this 3,400-acre bayside wilderness are unsurpassed. For something a bit closer in, have a look at the Port Aransas Island RV Resort at the corner of Avenue G and 6th Street. It too is within walking distance of the water.

Rockport

The only community of any size between the Aransas Pass–Port Aransas area and Aransas National Wildlife Refuge is Rockport. Located on SR 35 it is virtually the only place in which to spend the night if you want to get an early start toward the refuge. You can stay at any number of pleasant RV parks along the highway in town, or at Goose Island State Park twelve miles north. If you camp in the latter, visit the "Big Tree," a 2,000-year-old live oak said to be the largest tree in Texas. You also might want to tour the Fulton Mansion State Historical Structure, an ornate four-story French Second Empire-style house completed in 1876. The site is in the town of Fulton, ten minutes drive from Rockport.

One other structure I found interesting in the area was the Texas State Fishing Pier, spanning Copano Bay just north of town. The pier is so long that anglers carry their tackle, rods, kids, and dogs on grocery carts. The cost to dangle a minnow off the pier is quite modest, and there is plenty of free parking at either end.

Aransas National Wildlife Refuge

Only one sign points the way to Aransas National Wildlife Refuge, so don't miss it. The sign and the refuge entrance road—actually FM 774—are located on the east side of SR 35 about twenty miles north of Rockport. You'll turn east once again eight miles later onto FM 2040. Refuge headquarters is located on the edge of Aransas Bay another eight miles farther along. Be sure and stop at the visitor center to pay your entrance fee and to pick up a birder's checklist and refuge map.

Established in 1937 to protect the vanishing wildlife of coastal Texas, this 54,800-acre refuge offers visitors some of the most marvelous wildlife watching in the contiguous United States. Occupying the flat, heavily wooded Blackjack Peninsula, it is home to such large animals as deer, alligators, javelina, feral hogs, and cougars, plus more than 350 species of birds. Ringed by tidal marshes, blanketed with thick scrub, and broken by long, narrow creeks and sloughs, the peninsula's wetland-dryland habitat in combination with the temperate, subtropical climate of South Texas creates as nearly perfect a wild animal sanctuary as exists anywhere in the known world.

The best time to visit Aransas is between November and March when the great flights of migratory ducks, geese, and sandhill cranes—and smaller flights of rare whooping cranes—occupy the refuge in full force. I was there in early December and though plenty of waterfowl were in evidence, park rangers told me that only about half the usual complement of winter avians had arrived. The main tour road here is a paved, fifteen-mile-long loop that begins and ends at refuge headquarters. In addition to the primary route, there are several maintained walking trails in the backcountry as well as a centrally located observation tower from which visitors can observe and take pictures without being seen. The refuge is open from sunrise till sunset every day of the year.

Long-legged Statue.
One of Aransas's common visitors, a great blue heron stands motionless, trying to decide whether the photographer is edible or simply a nuisance.

Evening Camp on the Guadalupe.
Parked beneath a grove of hardwoods, this RVer enjoys a warm, lovely evening along the Guadalupe River just north of Tivoli.

Camping Near Aransas

Overnight stays in the refuge are prohibited by park policy, and one problem for RVers is that no campgrounds are available anywhere in the vicinity. The evening after I toured Aransas I stayed at Riverside Campground, just north of Tivoli on SR 35. Adjacent to the Guadalupe River, this pretty little riverbottom park caters mainly to fishermen who spend the entire winter, but certainly welcomes itinerant, one-night RVers as well. The camp is well shaded, and each site has a fire grill, picnic table, and all hookups.

POINTS OF INTEREST: Texas Tour 3

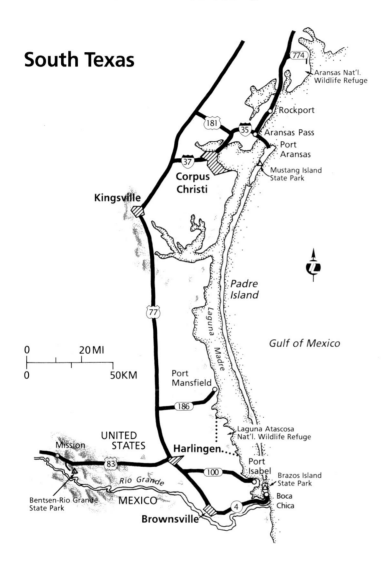

South Texas

Port Aransas: *Bill Fishing Tournaments* (sport fishing), March through October.

MUSEUMS & GALLERIES:

Mission: *South Texas Wildlife Museum and Gallery,* Tuesday–Saturday, 10 A.M.–5 P.M., mounted animals, dioramas, ranch artifacts, admission.

Brownsville: *Gladys Porter Zoo,* Ringgold and 6th streets, open every day 9 A.M. till dusk, rare and exotic animals in natural settings, admission; *Art League Museum,* 230 Neale Drive, open Monday, Wednesday, Thursday, and Friday, 9:30 A.M.–3:30 P.M., historic buildings and art exhibits; *Historical Museum,* 641 E. Madison, open Tuesday through Thursday, 1 P.M.–4 P.M., photo, history exhibits; *Stillman House Museum,* 1305 E. Washington, open Monday through Friday, 10 A.M.–12 P.M. and 2 P.M.–5 P.M., historical exhibits, admission.

Harlingen: *Confederate Air Force Museum,* Harlingen Airport, open Monday through Saturday 9 A.M.–5 P.M., Sunday and holidays 1 P.M.–6 P.M., antique planes, weapons, admission.

Kingsville: *Conner Museum,* 214 E. Kleberg, open Monday through Friday 9 A.M.–1 P.M., historic and King Ranch photos, exhibits.

Rockport: *Rockport Art Center,* Rockport Harbor, open Tuesday through Saturday, 10 A.M.–5 P.M., Sunday 2 P.M.–5 P.M., restored 19th-century home, gallery.

RESTAURANTS:

Mission: *Taco Olé,* 2316 N. Conway, Mexican food.

Brownsville: *Antonio's,* Strawberry Sq., Mexican food; *Resaca Club,* Fort Brown Hotel, 1900 E. Elizabeth, seafood, steaks.

South Padre Island: *Blackbeard's,* 103 East Saturn, seafood.

Port Aransas: *Island Cafe,* 224 Cotter, seafood, steaks.

Rockport: *Charlotte Plummer's,* Fulton Beach Rd., seafood.

ACCESS: *US 83* east from Mission; *US 77* north and south.

INFORMATION: *Mission Chamber of Commerce,* P.O. Box 431, Mission, TX 78572, (512) 585-2727; *Brownsville Chamber of Commerce,* P.O. Box 752, Brownsville, TX 78522, (512) 542-4341; *South Padre Island Tourist Bureau,* P.O. Box 3500, South Padre Island, TX, (800) 992-7263; *Confederate Air Force,* P.O. Box CAF, Harlingen, TX 78551, (512) 425-1057; *Rockport Chamber of Commerce,* P.O. Box 1055, Rockport, TX 78382, (512) 729-6445; *Port Aransas Tourist Bureau,* P.O. Box 356, Port Aransas, TX 78373, (512) 749-5919; *Aransas National Wildlife Refuge,* P.O. Box 100, Austwell, TX 77950, (512) 286-3559.

ANNUAL EVENTS:

Mission: *Poinsettia Show* (flower show with tropical theme), December.

Brownsville: *Charro Days* (four-day costume fiesta, parades, music, dancing), February.

Hill Country Trail, I

Central Texas in general, and the tree-covered Hill Country in particular, inconstant, are ever dependent on the sun's position and strength for their moods and colors. In the cool light of morning, the landscape glimmers like a soft, green bed of moss; at noon it swelters white hot, curling inward as if to say "too warm, too warm!" Evening finds it smiling, while rock, tree, twig, cow, and fencepost gleam golden red. And on cloudy days it glowers, displeasure of a grayish sort at the stingy light.

Carl Spencer,
Ode to an Oak Tree

Driving south through the "black earth" country of the Concho Valley toward San Angelo, I began to realize exactly what the term "wide open spaces" means. As a travel journalist I spend much of my time in foreign locales—Europe, Asia, South America—and there, space is at a premium. In many places, crammed together like bees in a hive, people must compete not only for room to live but simply to breathe.

In the backcountry of Texas, things are different. Folks have space to spare, space in which to move, to think, to ponder about life and whatever it means. Some visitors, of course, complain that the state is simply too big, too wide, too far away from everything ("Hell, ma'm, it's only a three-hour drive to the store"). I don't agree. Frankly I envy those who reside in this land of horizon-to-horizon sky, rusty barbed-wired fences longer than the island of Manhattan, and blacktop ribbons that may flow across the terrain for fifteen miles with neither dip nor curve.

Tour **4** *222 miles*

SAN ANGELO • FORT CONCHO • BRADY • MASON • FORT MASON • FREDRICKSBURG • ADMIRAL NIMITZ STATE HISTORICAL PARK • ENCHANTED ROCK STATE NATURAL AREA • KERRVILLE • LOST MAPLES STATE NATURAL AREA

San Angelo

I began the first leg of my Hill Country tour in San Angelo, a small, pretty, flatland city of 84,000, situated at the junction of US 67 and US 87. Once an early-day cattle- and sheep-ranching center, today local industries include the manufacture of oil-field equipment, plastics, medical supplies, and jet aircraft. There is a state university located here, and the city even has its own symphony orchestra.

There were two things that struck me immediately about San Angelo, both of them important to RVers. First, it is an extremely clean town; the smogless air sparkles with life, and buildings, homes, and streets are well kept and show few signs of decay. Second, RVers can move easily around the town. Traffic is generally light, the streets are wide, and directional signboards to San Angelo's main visitor attractions are posted everywhere.

Fort Concho

If you want to spend a night or two in San Angelo, there is a comfortable KOA traveler's park ("We Pamper the Camper") southwest of town on FM 584. Once you've had a good night's sleep, I recommend starting your tour of the city at old Fort Concho on Avenue D in the southeast section of town.

From 1878 until 1881, Fort Concho was headquarters for the Pecos Military District, and from here cavalry and infantry soldiers protected travelers and the U.S. mail from Indian and outlaw attack. Later in the century, as the frontier moved farther west, it was used as a base for surveying and mapping new territory. The fort was finally abandoned in 1889 when Washington declared it was no longer needed to protect the local citizens.

Cool and Shady.
The "black earth" country of the Concho Valley abounds with cool, quiet, and shady rivers. Many are filled with fish and virtually alive with songbirds and other wildlife.

Today this old garrison is among the best preserved of all Texas frontier military forts. In the huge headquarters building, constructed of limestone blocks and pecan wood, you'll find an excellent exhibit of antique firearms, as well as Indian relics from the San Angelo region and interesting historic photographs. Across the street from headquarters there is an exact restoration of a nineteenth-century cavalry barracks, complete with bunks, blankets, even the contents of soldiers' footlockers. In another part of the complex there are a stable, doctor's office, and a frontier store, all restored to perfect 1880s condition.

There is plenty of RV parking both in front of the headquarters building and on the streets adjacent to the fort. If you visit on a weekend, sign up for a Fort Concho tour led by tour guides dressed in period costumes. The guides are all local and are adept at explaining in detail how life was lived a century before.

Concho River Walk

The Concho River Walk is another place you'll want to see. An exquisite, six-mile-long riverside park and walkway built especially for joggers, bicyclers, and picnickers. Adjacent to the slow-flowing Concho River, smack

Down by the Riverside.
The Concho River Walk is a six-mile-long pathway that was built especially for joggers, bicyclers, and picnickers.

in the middle of downtown San Angelo, this verdant belt is a sanctuary for wildlife as well as city dwellers and visitors, and large numbers of birds are usually in evidence. In addition to lots of picnic sites, grassy shade, and scenic views of the river, the site also contains a small amusement park, a paddle-boat concession, and a nine-hole golf course. The easiest access for RVers is to turn east off US 87 onto Rio Concho Drive.

City Museums

The General Telephone Exhibit Museum on South Johnson Street offers visitors a unique display. Here you'll find almost every model of phone built in America—from Alexander Graham Bell's "Gallows Frame Phone" to ultramodern modulars. And on East Concho Street, browse through Miss Hattie's Museum, a restored bordello that, as the local chamber of commerce puts it, "was a surreptitious San Angelo landmark for decades." Miss Hattie's opened in the mid-1800s and operated continually until it was finally closed down by Texas Rangers in 1946.

Frog Pond Creek

There are several routes southeast into the Hill Country from San Angelo, but I recommend US 87 because of its directness and its scenic vistas. The landscape south of town is unlike any other region of Texas. Farms stretch into the distance as far as you can see. Every house has its own windmill, every field its tractor, every garden its bright little pocket of chrysanthemums, daisies, or roses. It could be Kansas, or Iowa, or even Ohio—only the accents are different.

Texas covers 275,416 square miles—large enough to fit fifteen of the fifty states within its borders and still have 1,000 square miles left over. It extends 801 straight-line miles from north to south and 773 miles from east to west.

Farm Country.
South of San Angelo on US 87, farms stretch into the distance as far as the eye can see.

Twenty miles south of San Angelo, US 87 crosses a small, boggy stream known as Frog Pond Creek. An unlikely cognomen to be sure, but this meandering waterway flowing through the edge of the Hill Country is famous. It was in this very spot a few years ago that the tale of the Rabbit and Snake began.

The story goes thusly: One day a blind rabbit and a blind rattlesnake, one hopping, the other slithering, came face to face in the thick mesquite brush along Frog Pond Creek.

"What the heck are you?" the startled rabbit asked.

"I don't know," replied the equally unsettled reptile. "I'm blind. What the heck are *you?*"

"I don't know," said the rabbit. "I'm blind too. Any suggestions?"

"Well," murmered the snake, "if you won't think I'm being fresh, I'll touch you. Maybe I can find a clue." At the rabbit's grunt of agreement, the rattlesnake carefully flickered out his tongue and felt the bunny's tiny cold nose, its twitching ears, soft fur, and short, powderpuff tail. "I know what you are!" it shouted excitedly. "You're a Texas jackrabbit!"

Tears ran down the hare's fuzzy face and onto the dry Texas earth. "After all these years," it blubbered. "Finally I have an identity."

"Now it's your turn," said the snake, impatiently. "I want an identity, too."

Wiping away its tears with one quivering paw, the rabbit reached out slowly and touched the reptile's body. "Hmmm," it murmured. "Let's see now. A scaly belly, two small beady eyes, a long, forked tongue. I've got it! You're a Texas lawyer!"

Live Oaks and Hill Country Blues

At the small, isolated town of Eden, you'll leave the farm country behind and head into the rolling oak-covered hills which mark the western boundary of the Texas Hill Country. It's difficult to corral this portion of the state into a single definition. The Hill Country is vast, encompassing several thousand miles in all, stretching from Fredonia in the north to Austin in the east, to San Antonio and Uvalde on the south and west. The land is rural and rugged, consisting of range upon range of low, rocky hills, thickly blanketed with juniper, willow, and the exquisite, black-trunked live oak. Culturally it is similar to the Ozarks or to Appalachia, though more sophisticated. The food here is Tex-Mex; the music, country and western; the basic philosophy, live and let live.

Most RVers, however, at least those who travel in the springtime, are far more interested in the Hill Country's wildflowers than they are its life-styles or heritage. Virtually thousands of tourists come here each April and May to observe, photograph, and generally gloat over the wonderful wildflower carpets that bloom profusely along the roadsides. Bluebonnets of "Hill Country Blues"—short, frizzy, blue flowers with white tips—are the most common, but there are hundreds of other species as well, many with far stranger names. Some, for instance—frog fruit, lizard tail gaura,

Roadside Bouquet.
Verbena is one of the most common wildflowers in the Hill Country.

goat head, buffalo gourd, and cardinal flower—are named for animals, while others like cheese weed, wild onion, and scrambled eggs are named for food. Then there are those dubbed by reputation—sneeze weed, loco weed, crazy weed, and crow poison. Finally, there is the "who-knows?" category. Here we find such anomalies as clammy plant, spectacle pod, snow-on-the-mountain, Mexican hat, and old plainsman.

If you plan to travel the Hill Country in the spring, I recommend obtaining a good book on Texas flora. A copy of *Flowers of Texas* is available free at any Texas Tourist Bureau office, or by writing the Department of Texas Parks and Wildlife at P.O. Box 5064, Austin, Texas 78763. One I like better though is *Wildflowers of the Llano Estacado* by Francis L. Rose and Russell W. Strandtmann, which can be purchased at almost any Texas bookstore.

Brady

First settled in the mid-1800s, the town of Brady lies just at the western edge of the Hill Country on the old Dodge Cattle Trail, seventy-six miles southeast of San Angelo. Nicknamed the "Heart of Texas," Brady is located just five miles southeast of the exact geographical center of the state.

Be sure to stop at the Heart of Texas Historical Museum to view the early ranch and home exhibits, antique farm implements, and old guns. Housed in a restored county jail, the museum still displays prisoner hardware and the musty cells used to restrain lawbreakers in frontier times.

Heart of Texas.
The Texas Historical Museum in Brady offers ranch and home exhibits and is housed in a restored county jail.

Mason

Similar to Brady in size, shape, and personality is the town of Mason, twenty-eight miles farther south on US 87. The main attraction for visitors here is old Fort Mason, a long-abandoned cavalry post atop the highest hill in town, where General Robert E. Lee was once commanding officer. It was, in fact, Lee's last U.S. Army duty station; he was called to Washington from Fort Mason, where he refused command of the Union Army being prepared for the Civil War.

Mason has two other historic structures worth a visit. One is the country museum, housed in a circa-1867 schoolhouse, and containing a number of artifacts from the old fort. The second is the Seaquist Home, a seventeen-room mansion (with fourteen fireplaces) built in the late 1880s. Both are open daily but you might need advance reservations to visit the Seaquist Home.

Fredricksburg

While Fredricksburg, Texas, might not be one of the liveliest communities in the state, it is certainly one of the prettiest. Settled by German immigrants in 1846, many of the other buildings in town retain a crisp, traditional German style, while the newer ones are always freshly painted. The downtown area consists of only one main street (Main Street, naturally), a wide, old-west-style avenue lined with antique shops, small cafés, bakeries, and quaint boutiques. Flowers bloom like newly emerged butterflies from wooden barrels along the shaded sidewalks. Backstreets are clean and quiet, most of them overhung with live oaks and hardwoods.

Admiral Nimitz State Historical Park

Fredricksburg offers numerous visitor attractions, but the largest and most popular is the Admiral Nimitz State Historical Park, located downtown in the old Steamboat Hotel. Five-star Admiral Chester Nimitz, commander-in-chief of Pacific Operations during World War II, was born in Fredricksburg in 1885. The museum, built in his honor, contains many of Nimitz's prized possessions, as well as some of the rarest artifacts of the war. Among the larger displays here is an art gallery exhibiting combat art and photographs, a lovely Japanese garden (presented to the museum by the people of Japan), and a hands-on history walk, lined with World War II aircraft, tanks, and ground weapons.

Enchanted Rock State Natural Area

Another popular place is Enchanted Rock State Natural Area, eighteen miles north of Fredricksburg on FM 965. This road, by the way, is as crooked as a dog's hind leg, winding through the oak-covered hills. The tough driving, however, is offset by the scenic beauty. Watch for deer and wild turkey, both numerous along the highway.

According to scientists, Enchanted Rock is part of a geologic region known as the Llano Uplift. The "rock" itself is a massive granite dome that

Enchanted Rock.
Eighteen miles north of Fredricksburg lies Enchanted Rock State Natural Area. Rising 500 feet into the air and covering about 70 acres, this massive granite dome was formed nearly a billion years ago.

rises 500 feet into the air and covers about 70 acres. It is one of the oldest visible rock exposures in the state and was formed during the Pre-Cambrian Era nearly a billion years ago.

Enchanted Rock has been utilized by Indians for virtually thousands of years (dart points and flint arrowheads are found frequently by visitors). Some tribes used it as a rallying point and meeting place, while others, so claim the legends, offered up human sacrifices to the spirits from the summit. Many Indians believed that ghost fires flickered from the dome's crest on moonlit nights, and all held the rock in reverence.

Today the park is a wonderful place in which to hike, picnic, or watch wildlife. The most popular walking trail at Enchanted Rock is a four-mile-long loop that circumnavigates the dome, beginning and ending at the visitor center. You can also walk (struggle) to the summit if you're in good condition; the trail climbs 425 feet in about six-tenths of a mile. If possible, I suggest visiting Enchanted Rock in late afternoon, when the dying sun turns the light-colored stone to silver. Camping here is restricted to small units (larger RVs can't turn around once they cross the bridge over Sandy Creek), but there's plenty of day-use parking near the visitor center.

Camping in Fredricksburg

There's a large KOA campground five miles east of Fredricksburg on US 290 at the junction of FM 1376, but many RVers prefer to stay in Lady Bird Johnson Municipal Park on SR 16, four miles south of town. I spent two nights here and was extremely pleased with the facilities and the atmosphere. The park straddles Live Oak Creek, and consists of 190 acres of

Lots of Live Oaks.
Lady Bird Johnson Municipal Park in Fredericksburg, four miles south of town on Live Oak Creek, is a popular RVers' campground.

trees and grass. There are nearly 100 fully equipped RV sites, a nine-hole golf course, putting greens, swimming pool, courts for volley ball, badminton, and tennis, and a twenty-acre, fish-filled lake.

Kerrville

From Fredricksburg, I headed southwest to Kerrville on SR 16, less than an hour's drive away. Texans would call SR 16 "a mighty pretty little highway," but you should be on the lookout for deer bounding onto the road from the roadside brush. Known as the "Deer Capital of the World," the white tail here are as numerous as flies on a dead hog. Adult deer aren't large (75 to 90 pounds) but hitting one at forty miles per hour will certainly damage your grill. It won't do much for the deer either.

Founded in the mid-1800s, the town of Kerrville, (population 17,000) has one of the most ideal climates in the United States. Temperatures are mild in both winter and summer, and it is a rare day when the sun doesn't shine. More than a dozen young people's camps, as well as scores of dude ranches and religious encampments, dot the picturesque valleys and oak-covered hills around the community, attracting virtually thousands of visitors each year.

Kerrville is also one of Texas's most important art centers, and if you happen to be in town on Memorial Day weekend, be sure to visit the annual Texas State Arts and Crafts Fair. And if you like western art, don't bypass the Cowboy Artists of America Museum on SR 173 south of town. A showcase for painters and sculptors such as Joe Beeler, John Clymer, Robert Duncan, and Gordon Snidow, this beautiful hilltop gallery offers not only a fine permanent collection but rotating shows as well. There's a great giftshop in the building where you can purchase signed or unsigned prints and lithographs.

Other Kerrville highlights are the Classic Car Showcase and Wax Museum, featuring a fleet of perfectly restored Duesenbergs, Bentleys, and Rolls-Royces and wax figures of their famous owners, and the Hill Country Museum with its antiques and artifacts from pioneer times in the region. Fishing is popular in the nearby Guadalupe River (they even teach it in school here), and if you want to stay a few days, check into Kerrville State Park on SR 173 South. Overlooking the Guadalupe River, the park encompasses 500 acres of grassy hills and timberland and offers all hookups, screened shelters, grills, and picnic tables. Nearby Flat Rock Lake contains crappie, catfish and largemouth bass; there's even a lighted fishing pier for night angling.

Lost Maples State Natural Area

State Route 39 heading west from Kerrville is so crooked it will knock your hat in the creek, but it is also one of the most scenic drives in the Hill Country. Winding in and out, up and down along the slow-flowing and emerald-green Guadalupe River, angling into the surrounding hills then back to the stream bed, it is reminiscent of a country lane through the Scottish Highlands. You won't average more than thirty-five miles per hour, but traffic is light so you can stop for pictures nearly anywhere.

If you turn south off SR 39 onto FM 187 about thirty miles from Kerrville, you'll be headed for Lost Maples State Natural Area, one of the least-utilized camping and recreation areas in the state. Nestled in a deep, twisting limestone canyon along the Sabinal River, this 2,200-acre park is named for the massive stands of bigtooth (canyon) maple that line the Sabinal riverbank and flow up the surrounding hillsides like an outgoing tide. These trees, by the way, are relatively unique; believed to be survivors of the Pleistocene Age, they are found only in a few Texas locations.

Lost Maples has just thirty campsites, and each is equipped only with water. Restrooms and showers, however, are handy, and a dump station is located near the visitor center. About ten miles of maintained hiking trails are found in the park where visitors may observe the overabundance of bird and other animal life that call Lost Maples home. Along with deer, bobcat, mountain lion, and Russian boar, the park is a sanctuary for bald and golden eagles, the rare golden-cheeked warbler, and the even rarer green kingfisher.

Wide Trails.
Hikers in Lost Maples will find wide, lovely trails, plenty of wildlife, and exceptional scenery in the backcountry.

A Pretty Drive.
State Route 39, just west of Kerrville,
which follows the Guadalupe River, is
one of the most scenic drives in the
Hill Country.

I heartily recommend that you park your rig in the campground, get out your hiking shoes and camera, take off your shirt, and spend a few pleasant days in Lost Maples. Sniff the wildflowers that grow throughout the park, talk to an armadillo, tread on a cactus, get a sunburn, maybe even walk off some of that excess baggage.

When you've done all that, you might want to day-trip into San Antonio, seventy miles to the east. I'm not overly fond of cities, but San Antonio is an exception. If nothing else I recommend visiting the Alamo (real name, Mission San Antonio de Valero) where 187 men including Davy Crockett, Bill Travis, and Jim Bowie fought to the last man in 1836, and the Alamo Museum where many relics from the famous battle are on display. Don't bypass a meander along the famous Paseo del Rio (the Riverwalk) in the downtown area, a half-hour-long riverboat taxi tour of the city or San Antonio's fabulous new Sea World. I also suggest that if you're hauling a tag-along, use it. Traffic is heavy in the nation's tenth largest city, and parking spaces for larger motorhomes are difficult to find.

On another day you might want to drive south to Uvalde and the Garner Memorial Museum, former home of John "Cactus Jack" Garner, vice president of the United States under Franklin D. Roosevelt. Return to Lost Maples by way of US 83, and at the junction of FM 337 in the town of Leakey, stop at Harvy and Jo Hulse's Wildlife Art Museum. Inside is an excellent collection of wildlife paintings, plus Harvy's personal collection of stuffed animals from all over the world.

POINTS OF INTEREST: Texas Tour 4

Hill Country Trail, I

0   20MI

0   50KM

ACCESS: *US 87 south from San Angelo.*

INFORMATION: *San Angelo Visitor's Information Center,* 500 Rio Concho Drive at Convention Center, San Angelo, TX 76903, (915) 655-4136; *Brady Chamber of Commerce,* 101 East First St., Brady, TX 76825, (915) 597-2420; *Mason Chamber of Commerce,* P.O. Box 156, Mason, TX 76856, (915) 347-5758; *Fredricksburg Chamber of Commerce,* P.O. Box 506, Fredericksburg, TX 78624, (512) 997-6523; *Enchanted Rock State Natural Area,* Route 4, Box 170, Fredericksburg, TX 78624, (915) 247-3903; *Kerrville Chamber of Commerce,* 1200 Sidney Baker St., Fredricksburg, TX 78028, (512) 896-1155; *Kerrville State Recreation Area,* 2385 Bandera Hwy., Kerrville, TX 78028, (512) 257-5392; *Lost Maples State Natural Area,* Station C Route, Vanderpool, TX 78885, (512) 966-3413.

ANNUAL EVENTS:

Kerrville: *Music Festivals* (live folk music and country/western), Memorial Day weekend, July 4th, Labor Day weekend; *Texas State Arts & Crafts Fair* (arts and crafts booths, exhibits), Memorial Day weekend, first weekend in June.

MUSEUMS AND GALLERIES:

San Angelo: *Fort Concho,* 213 East Ave. D, Monday–Saturday, 9 A.M.–5 P.M., Sunday, 1 P.M.–5 P.M., pioneer, cavalry artifacts; *General Telephone*

Exhibit Museum, 2701 South Johnson Street, Monday–Friday, 8 A.M.–5 P.M., early, present-day telephones; *Miss Hattie's Museum,* 18 East Concho, Tuesday–Saturday, 9:30 A.M.–4:30 P.M., bordello artifacts, relics, furnishings; *San Angelo Museum of Fine Arts,* Burgess Street at East Avenue G, Tuesday–Saturday, 10 A.M.–4 P.M., Sunday, 1 P.M.–4 P.M., changing exhibits.

Brady: *Heart of Texas Historical Museum,* corner of High and Main streets, open Saturday, Sunday, and Monday afternoons, farm and pioneer implements, vintage photographs.

Mason: *Mason County Museum,* 300 Moody Street, Monday–Friday, 9 A.M.–5 P.M., Fort Mason artifacts.

Fredricksburg: *Admiral Nimitz State Historic Site,* 340 East Main Street, 8 A.M.–5 P.M., daily except holidays, World War II exhibits, paintings, photographs; *Pioneer Museum,* 309 West Main St., daily April–October except Tuesday, 10 A.M.–5 P.M., pioneer implements.

Kerrville: *Cowboy Artists of America Museum,* 1550 Bandera Hwy. (SR 173), Tuesday–Saturday 9 A.M.–5 P.M., Sunday, 1 P.M.–5 P.M., rotating western art exhibits; *Hill Country Museum,* 226 Earl Garret St., Monday, 10 A.M.–12 P.M., 2 P.M.–4:30 P.M., Tuesday, Thursday, and Sunday, 2 P.M.–4:30 P.M., Hill Country artifacts, antiques; *Classic Car Showcase & Wax Museum,* FM 783, 10 A.M.–6 P.M. except Tuesday, Sunday, 12 P.M.–5 P.M., restored automobiles, wax figures of Hollywood celebrities.

RESTAURANTS:

San Angelo: *Zentner's Steak House,* 2715 Sherwood Way, steak and seafood.

Brady: *Charly's,* US 87 South, family-style steak and seafood.

Fredricksburg: *The Gallery,* 230 East Main, gourmet steak and seafood.

Kerrville: *The Acapulco,* 1718 Sidney Baker St., Mexican food; *Mamacita's,* 215 Junction Hwy, Mexican food.

LAND OF THE WILDFLOWERS
Hill Country Trail, II

Backward turn backward oh time with your
  wheel
Aeroplanes, wagons and automobiles
Dress me once more in sombrero that flaps
Spurs, flannel shirt, slicker, and chaps
Put a six shooter or two in my hand
Show me a yearling to rope and to brand
Out where the sage brush is dusty and gray
Make me a cowboy again for a day.

Author Unknown,
Life of a Cowboy

On a sunny spring morning, there is simply no place on earth prettier than the Texas Hill Country. Take an imaginary glance through the windsheld of my RV, for instance. Along the roadside, blooming in mixed clusters like a patchwork quilt, are thousands, *millions,* of wildflowers. Most common are bluebonnets, bright orange paintbrush, and the purplish verbena, but there are saw-leaf daisies, tansey asters, fireweels, and sunflowers as well. Just beyond the highway fence where the land begins to slope upward grow the ever-present, dark-green junipers, backlit in the morning sun. Farther up the hillsides are the canopied live oaks with blue-gray leaves; mixed among the oaks are lonely red-bud trees, bright splotches of crimson in a veritable sea of green. Then, at the ridgeline, the blue, knock-your-eyes-out, all-encompassing Texas sky hovers silently. Photographs and oil paintings do not do the scene proper justice; to believe, one has to see for oneself.

Tour 5 *227 miles*
Side trip to Austin, 58 miles

LOST MAPLES STATE NATURAL AREA • BANDERA • BOERNE • GUADALUPE RIVER STATE PARK • CANYON LAKE • AUSTIN • LONGHORN CAVERN STATE PARK • INKS LAKE STATE PARK

Leaving Lost Maples

My leg muscles sore and knotted from several days of trail exploration in Lost Maples State Natural Area, I left the park early and drove south on FM 187 to Vanderpool. From there I turned east onto FM 337 and headed back into the heart of the Hill Country.

Like most Hill Country backroads, FM 337 is twisty and slow—a thirty-five-mile-per-hour highway at best. In addition to the numerous curves, there are steep grades as well, so stay alert. If your rig is more than twenty feet long, you'll have to do plenty of gearing down.

The morning I drove the road, the local population of white-tailed deer were having a convention. I could see them by the score in the roadside brush, browsing cautiously on wildflowers and nervously flipping their white flags up and down. Turkey vultures (or buzzards) are other creatures common to this segment of the Hill Country. You'll see them on almost every fencepost or tall tree—large, black birds with purplish-red crowns—waiting patiently for something to die of its own free will, or better yet, to get squashed by a tourist.

One might say that vultures are nature's garbage cans. Unable to capture and kill their own prey because of unusual foot construction (their claws will not grasp), they live basically on carrion—dead, rotting animals that have been killed by others. Able to strip large animals of their flesh in a few days and smaller ones in a few hours, buzzards are a major aid in disease control, say biologists. They are well equipped for the job: Toxic strains of bacteria that might be encountered while feeding are killed by a vulture's digestive tract; head and neck are naked so that parasites and other organisms that cling to the skin will be destroyed by the ultraviolet rays of sunlight. They aren't pretty, but when you see one,

Fields of Flowers.
In the spring, fields of verbena are common sights along the Hill Country trail. Like soft, fuzzy, purple carpets, they seem to virtually cover the hillsides in places.

give it a word of thanks. Hill Country roads would be virtually littered with the carcasses of dead, fetid animals if it were not for these great, gloomy birds.

Bandera

At the town of Medina I turned east on SR 16 toward Bandera, also known as the "Cowboy Capital of the World." Founded in 1853 by Mormon settlers, today it is a small but lively resort community, restored as closely as possible by town fathers to its "frontier-days" look and style.

Bandera's hub is the historic county courthouse, constructed in 1890 and a masterpiece of hand-quarried, hand-laid limestone. If you have time, stop at the Frontier Times Museum on 13th Street, where you'll find a treasure house of frontier antiques including old-time spinning wheels, music boxes, oxen yokes, branding irons, and various other pioneer relics. There's an antique bottle collection here too (some are thought to have come from Judge Roy Bean's saloon in Langtry), as well as a fine display of old cap-and-ball pistols and muzzle-loading rifles.

If you're thinking about staying a day or two in town to savor the western flavor, camp at the Hill Country State Natural Area, located ten miles west of Bandera on FM 1077. The sanctuary consists of 5,300 acres; RV camping is primitive and allowed only on a 20-acre site in the park, but the scenic views and wildlife watching are spectacular.

At Home on the Range

Bandera's biggest claim to fame is the fact that it is the "Cowboy Capital of the World," or the "Dude Ranch Capital of the World," depending upon whom you ask. Surrounding this little burg are at least a dozen guest ranches offering accommodations that range from luxurious suites to a cot in a bunkhouse.

A couple of years ago I had the pleasure of spending a few days at one of these "instant cowboy" ranches. One highlight during my stay was taking part in an old-time cattle drive where guests actually lived and worked on the range, much like real cowpokes did a hundred years before. I remember that first day clearly. I arrived at the resort in early afternoon, then was driven—along with a few other dudes—to the site of the drive. After being introduced to the crew and the horses we would be responsible for (and hopefully learn to ride), we had dinner—a routine, everyday cowboy meal of honey-baked chicken, herbed rice, sourdough biscuits, salad, strawberry shortcake, and iced tea. After a few songs around the gas stove, we were led past the brightly painted chuck wagon accompanying the drive to our "cowboy bedrolls," large squares of heavy white canvas, two-inch-thick foam pads, and three itchy wool blankets each, all folded together in an intricate and secret pattern understood only by the Great Wrangler in the Sky.

To utilize a cowboy bedroll in the proper manner, I found out during the next few minutes, one had to be persistent. Step number one: Lay it

Move Em' Out!
Cowboys for a day watch over a herd of cattle while on a Bandera cattle drive.

out on level ground away from trees (lightening), holes in the ground (rattlesnakes, spiders, and rodents), and rocks (midnight anguish). Step number two: Remove clothing and new high-heeled boots, then crawl into the narrow opening at one end, taking all but the boots with you in case of rain. Try not to relocate gravel, leaves, or wayward insects in the process. Step number three: Use a saddle blanket for a pillow, and hope for the best. It required at least twenty minutes of kicking and struggling to maneuver myself into a comfortable position inside the bedroll's bowels, and another ten for the moans and curses of discomfort from others to finally cease.

Early the next morning we were awakened in the predawn silence by the muffled thumping of hooves on the far side of the chuck wagon. A frantic voice shouted "Whoa!" I noticed a few heads appear from the bedrolls; someone muttered "Whazzat?" Then the hoofbeats ceased. Heads disappeared, back into the warmth of the canvas and wool cocoons.

Suddenly the shouts and trampling noises began again, this time much closer. Heads appeared once more, and several of the bedrolls began to slither for safety beneath the chuck wagon. One collided with a wagon wheel; another knocked over the coffee pot and set it clattering along the ground. There was one final "Whoa!" then silence.

"Mornin'," said Randall Johnson, foreman of the crew we had met the afternoon before. He was also one of three cowboys who trotted around the chuck wagon's rear fender, holding the reins of make-believe horses and stomping their boots into the rock earth. "Dang broncs is always a little antsy this early," Johnson drawled. "Rise and shine, we got a long

Chow Down!
Gathered around a campfire, dude-
ranch guests and working cowboys on a
Bandera cattle drive wait for dinner to
be served.

day ahead." He galloped off, though not fast enough to escape a dried cow
pie that hurtled from beneath the chuck wagon and sent his Stetson
flying.

It was Randall Johnson's job to keep us greenhorns (someone who
doesn't know which end of a cow to milk) from being trampled, snakebit-
ten, gored, or otherwise mutilated during our one-and-a half days on the
drive. "Them cows is fully growed and ornery," he told us over a breakfast
of bacon, eggs, and hotcakes. "Ever' one of 'em is as mean as a one-eyed
rattlesnake when they're tired. Don't let no grass grow under yer horse,
keep them cows movin', and keep 'em in line. Otherwise we'll have kettle
(the kind you grow on a kettle wrench) scattered all over the Hill
Country."

The "kettle," about eighty of them, were contained for the moment in a
small holding pasture a short distance from camp. They were longhorn
steers, unpredictable, jumpy, and according to every cowboy legend I'd
ever heard, potentially dangerous. The cowboys accompanying us were
authentic, too, each a genuine working cowpoke, able to sit on a horse at
full gallop while rolling a cigarette with one hand and playing a guitar

with the other. (The fellow who told me that immediately pulled a dusty toothbrush from a shirt pocket and began to brush his teeth. "Gotta git the taste of all them lies outta my mouth," said he.) All of them looked pretty much alike—tall, rangy young men, dressed in weathered, wide-brimmed hats, checkered shirts, and blue jeans stuffed into dusty, high-topped boots. Their faces were tanned, the color fading to a field of pale at the shirt collar. To their upper lips were attached large, drooping moustaches; lower lips were pouched with plugs of chewing tobacco.

We were underway by 8 A.M. At three miles per hour the herd of cattle hurtled through the Darwinian macrocosm of Hill Country vegetation, eating much of it as they went and thoroughly trampling the rest. With no idea of just how mean a "one-eyed rattlesnake" could be, most of us greenhorns played cowboy cautiously, trying to remember the instructions given us at breakfast. Clockwise around the herd (we were told) there was to be one rider at "point," two at right "swing," two more at right "flank," three at "drag," and so on up the other side. Point set speed and direction; swing and flank kept the strays contained as the herd moved forward; drag, traditionally the least desired position on a drive because of the dust, was the moving force, prodding the slowpokes along with a concerto of whistles, yelps, and yips. Thus was a herd of kettle surrounded, led, pushed, and embraced.

To make this long, dusty story shorter by several thousand curses, we finally drove the herd into a small meadow in late afternoon where they could water in a nearby stream and graze throughout the night. Our horses were unsaddled, fed, and watered, then tethered nearby. As the beautiful Hill Country evening rolled in over the thick stands of live oak, we said goodby to the cowboys and boarded a pickup truck for the ride back to the ranch. On the way, someone began to sing a less-than-romantic trail's-end ballad we had learned the night before. Glad to be alive, we all joined in:

> I'm up in the morning afore daylight
> and afore I sleep the moon shines bright.
> No chaps and no slicker, and it's pouring down rain.
> And I swear by God, that I'll never night herd again.
> Oh, it's bacon and beans most every day,
> I'd as soon be a-eatin' prairie hay.
> I went to the boss to draw my roll.
> He had it figured out I was nine dollars in the hole.
> I'll sell my horse and I'll sell my saddle;
> You can go to hell with your longhorn cattle.

Boerne

From Bandera, I followed SR 16 to the town of Pipecreek, then to escape the San Antonio traffic I turned north on SR 46 toward Boerne. There are a couple of things you might want to do in this old German community of 4,300. One is to visit the Cave Without a Name, located six miles northeast of town on FM 474. When the cave opened to visitors in 1939, local

Horse d'Oeuvres.
A cattle-drive cook serves a platter of appetizers to hungry cowboys.

Old Hand.
On a Bandera cattle drive, an old timer drives the chuck wagon that carries food and bedrolls for guests.

townspeople thought it too pretty to name, so they didn't. Inside, stalagmites, stalactites, and dozens of other formations hang from the roof or bloom from the walls and floor. If you like classic religious buildings, stop at St. Peter's Church on South Main. If you arrive in time for lunch, picnic in the shade in the city park on SR 46 East. Afterward, tour the Agricultural Heritage Center, featuring indoor and outdoor exhibits of antique farm machinery and equipment. The center is adjacent to the city park. Boerne, by the way is pronounced Bur-nee; the original village here was Tusculum (named for Roman statesman Cicero's country home), and was founded in 1849 by members of the idealist colony of Beltina, students of the classics who founded several "Latin settlements" in Texas.

Guadalupe River State Park

The entrance road to Guadalupe River State Park lies thirteen miles east of Boerne on SR 46. Consisting of 1,900 acres of forest, mainly sycamore, elm basswood, and persimmon trees, the park straddles the Guadalupe River about three miles north of the main highway.

A Lovely Canyon.
Eons of erosion have carved the limestone walls of this Guadalupe River State Park canyon into a photographer's dream.

The RV campground is hidden away in the trees a few hundred yards from the river. There are forty-eight sites with hookups here, and each is segregated from its neighbors by a thick screen of trees and undergrowth. The basic park activities include canoeing and swimming in the Guadalupe River, as well as hiking and birdwatching.

The river itself, its banks lined with huge, bald cypress trees, is perhaps the park's most outstanding natural feature. Green and slow flowing, it glides east through the towering limestone bluffs of the Edwards Plateau, a perfect stream for nature-watching canoeists and hikers. You'll notice an interesting phenomenon on the riverbank below the campground, however, reminding us that quiet rivers have a way of suddenly changing face. In 1978, more than thirty inches of rain fell on the Texas Hill Country. As it did, the Guadalupe flooded, cresting out at sixty-three feet above the normal stream level. The rushing water carried massive rafts of timber and trash downstream, snapping the tops off riverside cypress like tooth-picks. Today you can still see the results of the flood in the canyon bottom. The surviving cypress lean desperately downstream, permanently deformed by the tremendous force of rushing water. In daylight the bent and twisted shapes make for excellent pictures; at night, they are down-right spooky.

Deformed Majesty.
A giant cypress, stripped of soil around its roots by Guadalupe River flood waters, guards the riverbank in the park.

Canyon Lake

Nearby Canyon Lake is a 12,000-acre flood-control reservoir located just east of US 281 between FM 2673 and FM 306. I got lost a couple of times trying to find it and finally discovered that the best access is from Sattler near the lake's southeast corner. From Sattler, follow FM 2673 northeast to its junction with FM 306 and turn left. A number of well-marked lake-access roads branch off FM 306 to the west.

Canyon Lake is one of the Hill Country's best fishing and watersports lakes, and to handle the crowds that show up on weekends, the Corps of Engineers has constructed half a dozen pretty little camping areas here. Most have only water hookups, but dump stations are available at each site as are restrooms and showers. Jacobs Creek Park, Canyon Park, and Potters Creek Park lie on the lake's east and north shores, while Cranes Mill Park and Comal Park are on the west. If you plan to do any side-trip exploring in this part of the Hill Country, Canyon Lake is an excellent hub. And naturally, the springtime wildflowers around the reservoir are spectacular.

Wildlife Wilderness

One nearby attraction you don't want to miss is the Wildlife Wilderness Drive Thru Ranch, an exotic animal sanctuary located seven miles east of Sattler on FM 306. The road through the ranch is only about 2½ miles long but might take all morning to drive, depending upon your supply of film. Some of the critters you'll see grazing or sleeping in the oak forest

State Capitol Complex.
Located on forty-six manicured acres in the center of town, Austin's State Capitol Complex is the city's major visitor attraction.

are Indian black buck, zebra, axis deer, oryx, and eland. On the way out, stop at the "petting pen" at ranch headquarters. Both white-tailed deer and Australian emu wander free, greeting tourists and begging a pat or a nibble.

Side Trip to Austin

Since the Texas capital city of Austin was a place I'd never been but heard much about, I decided to chance the traffic and spend a couple of days sightseeing. The quickest way to reach Austin from Canyon Lake is to follow FM 306 east to its junction with I-35 and turn north. The drive from the junction takes about an hour.

On the southern outskirts of town I checked into the Austin KOA, located just a block from the interstate. I personally don't care for private campgrounds because they tend to be more expensive. This campground is, however, comfortable and quiet, offering about 100 sites, a swimming pool, grocery store, propane, and a recreation center. And adjacent to the interstate, it provides easy access to most of Austin's attractions.

Founded in 1839, Austin is a beautiful, manicured city, without a doubt the most attractive metropolitan area in Texas. It is also compact, and, even with 400,000 people residing inside the city limits, quite easy to maneuver in an RV.

Your first stop should be the State Capitol Complex, forty-six acres of immaculate, landscaped grounds straddling a hill in the center of town. The statehouse, similar to the U.S. Capitol Building in Washington, D.C., is massive, constructed of Texas pink granite and rising from the surrounding gardens and trees like a great, extemporaneous sentinel. Free guided tours are offered daily from 8:30 A.M. till 4:30 P.M., and the Capitol Tourist Information Center is open seven days a week.

There are eight major city parks in Austin encompassing more than 5,000 acres of trees, lakes, rivers, and grass. Park facilities include four golf courses, tennis courts, athletic fields, and swimming pools. Speaking of swimming, be sure to visit Barton Springs, located in Zilker Park in southwest Austin. This natural stone swimming pool, fed by icy spring water welling naturally from the ground, is a great place in which to do your morning laps.

Other things you might wish to see and do include a riverboat tour of the city aboard the paddle-wheeler *Lone Star* (departing from the Hyatt Regency Hotel), a trip through the famous Austin Nature Center, or a tour of the home of short story writer O. Henry (real name William Sydney Porter). Austin also boasts several excellent museums, among them the George Washington Carver Museum of Black History and Culture, the Harry Ransom Center with its 1455 Gutenberg Bible and photography exhibits, and the Texas Memorial Museum featuring historical and archaeological exhibits. For a bird's-eye view of the city, drive to the top of Mount Bonnell at Austin's western edge; vistas here of the surrounding Hill Country are breathtaking. And for a morning's hike, try McKinney Falls State Park (you can also camp overnight here), thirteen miles to the southeast just off Scenic Loop Road. Trails meander from rapid to waterfall to deep, quiet pool along the stream, and birdlife in the canopy of overhanging trees is extensive.

Downtown Austin.
There are plenty of skyscrapers in this attractive Texas city, but Austin still exudes a small-town atmosphere.

Northwest to Longhorn Cavern

I got turned around several times leaving Austin because of poorly marked streets in the southwest part of the city. My vagabond temperament prevailed, however, and I finally escaped the traffic and returned to the rural Hill Country via US 290/71. Where the two highways split, I stayed on US 71, following the Colorado River toward Lyndon B. Johnson Lake. Five miles north of the town of Marble Falls, I turned west on scenic Park Road 4 to Longhorn Cavern State Park.

Virtually hundreds of limestone caves exist in the Texas Hill Country, but Longhorn Cavern is considered to be the most scenic by far. Officially designated as a state park in 1932, it covers more than 600 acres of rugged and rocky terrain on what is locally known as Backbone Ridge. The cavern itself was carved in limestone some 450 million years ago by the turbulent forces of an exhausted inland sea. Fossil remains indicate that the cave was once home to a variety of critters, among them bats and large beasts of prey. Early humans used it as well, leaving their flint arrowheads and spear points near the entrance. During the Civil War, Longhorn was used as a Confederate stronghold and gunpowder factory, and rumors claim that outlaw Sam Bass once used it as a hideout in between train robberies and other illegal forays.

Spelunkers and cave archaeologists have explored about eleven miles of the cavern but its exact length is unknown; some scientists think it may even be connected to Carlsbad Caverns several hundred miles to the west. The guided visitor tours are only about 1¼ miles in length, but are certainly worth the effort. You'll meander leisurely between the slender, cool, white limestone walls, dropping from surface level to 120 feet below the ground at an easy rate, even for children. Stalagmites and stalactites are rare, but you'll see such natural wonders as a naturally carved bust of Abraham Lincoln, a giant footprint, and the amazing Hall of Gems (where the walls gleam as if covered with diamonds). The cavern's temperature is always a comfortable 64°, and the tour takes less than two hours.

Above ground, there's a museum displaying Indian artifacts found in the area and several Civil War relics discovered in the cavern itself. Overnight camping isn't allowed in the park, but picnicking and hiking are.

Tour's End—Inks Lake

I ended my 450-mile-long sojourn through the Texas Hill Country at Inks Lake, a 1,200-acre state park lying six miles north of Longhorn Cavern on Park Road 4. Created in the 1930s and today a manicured combination of cedar and oak woodlands, pink granite hills, deep, cool lakes, and slow-moving rivers, the park is a great spot to rest and recreate for a few days. Wildlife is profuse in the forest, and recreational attractions here include boating, canoeing, water skiing, sailing, fishing, and even scuba diving.

Inks Lake has a number of RV campgrounds, all with electricity and water and most of them located adjacent to a lake or stream. There's a nine-hole golf course on the property, and you can rent fishing boats or canoes from a shop at the public boat ramp. Because of its proximity to the massive U.S. Army base at Fort Hood and the city of Austin, the park is often crowded on weekends. During the week, however, you'll virtually have the place to yourself.

If you want to explore the area a bit, several points of interest—most of them requiring little more than a few minutes by car to reach—can be found nearby. Ten minutes away in Burnet, for example, there's Old Fort Croghan, an 1849 army outpost established to protect local settlers against Indian attack. In Burnet's Pioneer Museum, you can examine an expansive collection of frontier artifacts, and south of town off US 281 is Old Mormon Mill, a small furniture-building community established in 1851 by Mormon settlers but abandoned two years later because of harassment by Indians.

At Kingsland, located on FM 1431 between Granite Shoals and Buchanan Dam, take a pontoon boat excursion on Lyndon B. Johnson Lake. These narrated trips offer plenty of wildlife watching and some nice views of the reservoir. You can catch the boat at the Colorado River Bridge on FM 1431 south of town. This narrow farm road, by the way, is extremely scenic, especially in the spring. Wildflower displays here in April and May are among the best in the state.

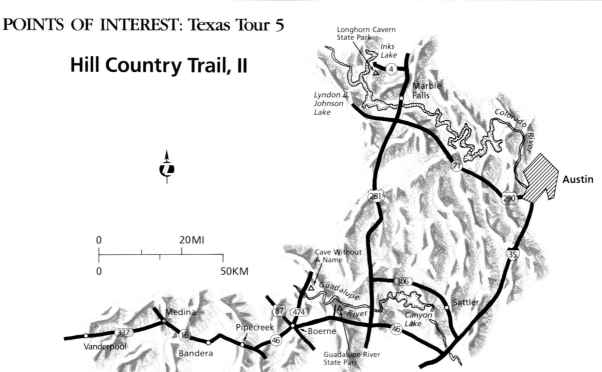

POINTS OF INTEREST: Texas Tour 5

Hill Country Trail, II

ACCESS: From Lost Maples State Natural Area, drive north and east on *FM 337, SR 46, FM 306, Interstate 35, US 281* and *US 71.*

INFORMATION: *Bandera County Chamber Of Commerce,* P.O. Box 171, Bandera, Texas 78003, (512) 796-4312; *Boerne Chamber of Commerce,* 1209 South Main, Boerne, TX 78006, (512) 249-9373; *Guadalupe River State Park,* Park Road 31, Route 2, Box 2087, Bulverde, TX 78163, (512) 438-2656; *Canyon Lake Reservoir Manager,* Star Route 3, Box 400, New Braunfels, TX 78130 (write only); *Austin Chamber of Commerce,* 901 West Riverside Drive, Austin, Texas 78744, (512) 478-9383; *Longhorn Cavern State Park,* Route 2, Box 23, Burnet, TX 78611, (512) 756-6976; *Inks Lake State Park,* Box 117, Buchanan Dam, TX 78609, (512) 793-2223.

ANNUAL EVENTS:

Bandera: *Frontier Days* (parade and cowboy festivities), Memorial Day weekend; *Old Time Rancher's Rodeo,* second weekend in August; *Labor Day Parade and PRCA Rodeo,* Labor Day; *Bandera County Fair,* autumn, dates vary. *Shoppers Jubilee* (Christmas Parade), first Friday in December.

Austin: *Aqua Festival* (parades, pageants, and contests), August.

MUSEUMS & GALLERIES:

Bandera: *Frontier Times Museum,* 506 13th St., Monday–Saturday, 10 A.M.–12 noon, 1 P.M.–4:30 P.M., Sunday, 1 P.M.–4:30 P.M., frontier exhibits; *Old Jail Museum & Art Gallery,* one block east of Texas 16 and Main Street junction, daily 10 A.M.–5 P.M., paintings, frontier artifacts.

Boerne: *Historical House Museum,* 402 Blanco St., Thursday, 2 P.M.–5 P.M., local history exhibits; *Agricultural Heritage Center,* SR 46 adjacent to city park, Sunday 1 P.M.–5 P.M., antique farm machinery.

Austin: *Laguna Gloria Art Museum,* West 35th St. at Old Bull Creek Road, Tuesday–Saturday, 10 A.M.–5 P.M., Sunday, 1 P.M.–5 P.M., changing exhibitions of 20th-century art; *Harry Ransom Center,* 21st and Guadalupe streets, Monday–Friday, 9 A.M.–5 P.M., Saturday, 9 A.M.–1 P.M., paintings, photography exhibits; *George Washington Carver Museum,* 1165 Angelina St., Monday, Tuesday, 9 A.M.–6 P.M., Thursday through Saturday, 1 P.M.–5 P.M., black history and culture exhibits; *Daughters of Confederacy and Daughters of Republic of Texas Museums,* Old State Land Office Building on grounds of State Capitol, 11th St. and Brazos. Confederacy museum Monday–Friday, 9 A.M.–5 P.M., DRT museum Wednesday–Saturday 10 A.M.–5 P.M., memorabilia from Civil War; *O. Henry Home,* 409 East 5th St., Tuesday–Saturday, 11 A.M.–4 P.M., Sunday, 2 P.M.–4:30 P.M.; *Texas Memorial Museum,* 2400 Trinity St., Monday–Friday, 9 A.M.–5 P.M., Saturday and Sunday, 1 P.M.–5 P.M.

RESTAURANTS:

Bandera: *O.S.T.* (Old Spanish Trail), Main St., Tex-Mex food.

Boerne: *Victoria's,* 123 West Blanco, elegant dining, lunch only; *Country Spirit,* 707 South Main, family-style American.

Austin: *Threadgill's,* 6416 North Lamar, home-style American; *Iron Works Barbecue,* 100 Red River, Texas barbecue.

Big Thicket Loop

The Big Thicket is still thick, and its depths are still as mysterious and forbidding as they were when the first settler came to live on corn and sweet potatoes, bear meat, and venison. The little, black, angry bees still hive in the hollows, and the buck deer leave their big scrapes on the dim woods trails. . . . And if you are desperate enough, here is one last place where you can find a hiding place till the trouble blows over.

Francis Abernethy,
Tales from the Big Thicket

The people who live in and around the Big Thicket region of East Texas claim it is the wildest, most uncivilized piece of territory in the contiguous United States, bar none. After spending a week exploring the densely forested backroads of the "Thicket" as it's simply known, I fully agree with that claim. Lying seventy-five or so miles north of Houston between I-45 and the Louisiana border, this land of tangled trees and gloomy hollows, of swamp, panther, bear, poisonous snake, and tall tale, is as unmarred by human endeavor today as it was 200 years ago. It is also one of the prettiest areas in all of Texas, especially during the moderate weather of spring and fall. I would hope that if you go nowhere else in the Lone Star State, at least visit the Big Thicket country; it is a place that no RVer should miss.

Tour 6 *227 miles*
Side trip to Galveston, 108 miles

HUNTSVILLE • HUNTSVILLE STATE PARK • SAM HOUSTON NATIONAL FOREST • POINT BLANK • LIVINGSTON • ALABAMA-COUSHATTA INDIAN RESERVATION • BIG THICKET • SARATOGA • GALVESTON

Huntsville

I began my own RV odyssey through the primeval forests of the Thicket in Huntsville, a small attractive city of 30,000, straddling I-45 in the northwest corner of the Sam Houston National Forest. Founded in 1831, the town originated as an Indian trading post—a tiny, isolated settlement where local Indian families could barter with American merchants for the white man's beads, mirrors, metal, and cloth.

Huntsville's most famous resident was Sam Houston, commander in chief of the Texas Army, first president of the Republic of Texas, and later a governor of the state. Houston died here in 1863, and his grave in Oakwood Cemetery is one of the town's most popular tourist attractions. If you would like to know more about the life and times of Houston, pay a visit to the Sam Houston Museum on Sam Houston Avenue, just across the street (naturally) from Sam Houston State University. The museum contains many of Houston's personal effects and is certainly worth a few hours of your time.

Huntsville State Park

On the advice of some RVing friends, I spent the night at Huntsville State Park, 2,000 acres of hardwoods and pines eight miles south of town just west of I-45. I arrived on Saturday afternoon, but the lovely tree-blanketed campground was virtually deserted. After checking in at the small visitor center, I parked in a quiet, shady space overlooking Lake Raven and spent the remainder of the afternoon watching the lake's contingent of wild ducks and alligators.

It's a wonderful place to stay if you plan on making day trips into the surrounding piney woods. There are several maintained nature trails that wander through the park, as well as a children's playground, boat-

Tangled Trees.
A land of tangled trees and gloomy hollows, of swamp, panther, bear, poisonous snake, and tall tale, the Big Thicket is one of the most rugged landscapes in North America.

launching ramp, and picnic area. Altogether Huntsville has about 200 campsites, although about half are strictly for tent campers and backpackers. The RV sites have full hookups.

Sam Houston National Forest

I awoke next morning to the musical chatter of thousands of piney woods songbirds. Returning to Huntsville via I-45, I turned east onto US 190 (exit 116) and entered the Sam Houston National Forest portion of the Big Thicket country a few miles outside of town.

There is only one way to describe the tree-covered landscape of the Sam Houston forest—thick! Grove after grove of loblolly and shortleaf pine, sweetgum, red maple, sassafras, dogwood, and various species of oak cover the rolling hills while river birch, water oak, black gum, and green ash flourish in profusion along the numerous creeks and bayous. Growth here is so unbelievably heavy, in fact, that only on a road or maintained forest trail can humans breach this solid wall of wood. Birdlife—everything from tiny wrens to wild turkeys—is incredibly abundant, and

Sam Houston Rode Here.
US 190 east of Huntsville runs through the lovely rolling hills of the Sam Houston National Forest.

the forest is alive with white-tailed deer by the thousands, opossums, raccoons, armadillos, wild hogs, and even black bears.

Traditionally, of course, it was this impenetrable barrier of timber that kept civilization at bay in East Texas, and it is still true today. The few communities along US 190 look as though they might have stepped right out of the 1930s. Ramshackle gas stations with five-decade-old gasoline pumps in front are common sights; weathered shacks and dilapidated barns slumber in tiny meadows that were probably cleared of timber before the Civil War occurred. Yards are littered with junk—rusty cars, broken washing machines, discarded clothing. And everywhere along the highway, small hand-lettered signs tacked to roadside trees tell stories of their own: *Ernie's Garage—We Work on Anything; Toasters Toilets Automobiles—We Butcher Hogs; We Have Chickens We Have Eggs; Beechnuts and Old Car for Sale Cheap.*

Point Blank

Half an hour's drive east of Huntsville, I stopped for breakfast at Miss Emily's in the village of Point Blank (population 325). As the friendly waitress served my heaping plate of eggs, sausage, hashbrowns, and biscuits with gravy, I asked her how the town had come by its unusual name. She thought for a moment, then turned toward an elderly man dressed in coveralls sitting by himself at a nearby table. "Fella over here wants to know how come we got a weird handle," she shouted, loud enough to be heard in Huntsville. "You hep 'em, Alton?"

The man got up, walked to my table, and introduced himself as Alton Knight, jack-of-all trades presently retired, and lifelong resident of Point Blank. "This here used to be a bootleg community," Knight drawled over his coffee. "They was stills and illegal whisky all over the county. One night a couple of them bootleggers was murdered down the road a piece . . . with a shotgun. Kinda messy I guess. Anyway, they named the place Point Blank cause that's what range them fellas was shot at."

I asked Knight if there were still illegal liquor operations operating in the neighborhood. He gave me a sly look, then glanced over his shoulder, presumably in search of lurking "revenooers."

"A few still around," he said softly. "Feds got one just down the road last week."

The simple fact is, I came to find out later, that the making of illegal liquor or "white lightning" is still big business in East Texas, and especially around the Big Thicket. Strangely enough, however, it isn't made for reasons of economy, since the cost of bootlegged whiskey is far greater than what one would pay in a store for bourbon or Scotch. Instead, the creation of white lightning is one of those traditions that has survived for 200 years, simply because it *is* a tradition and isn't about to die just because a group of federal authorities say it must. Frankly, it's surprising that white lightning still exists; as Alton Knight told me, "The dang stuff will burn the lining right outta yor mouth."

There are 23.4 million acres of woodlands in Texas of which 10.9 million acres are the pine-hardwood forests (Piney Woods) in the eastern portion of the state. Extensive forests can be found in 43 of the state's 254 counties.

Breakfast Browsing.
Two young white-tailed deer browse quietly in the thick woodlands near Point Blank.

Livingston

Three miles past Miss Emily's, I crossed the bridge spanning one arm of massive Lake Livingston, passed through the bustling lakeside burg of Onalaska, and stopped twenty minutes later at the Polk County Museum in the town of Livingston. Inside, I discovered a very viewable collection of Early American glassware, rare stamps, old coins, and regional Indian relics. The museum's pride and joy is a circa-1700 candelabrum that graced the White House for years. And near the museum is another of Livingston's historic attractions—the Jonas Davis log cabin. Hauled piece by piece from deep in the piney woods where it sat for more than 100 years, the ancient structure has been re-erected by local residents in the downtown area. I couldn't help but wonder as I examined the old cabin if people still lived in similar buildings in the surrounding woods.

I spent the night on the shores of the lake at Lake Livingston State Park, a 640-acre recreation site seven miles southwest of town. Surrounded by forest, this is an excellent place to stay while exploring the Livingston area. Facilities include hookups, screened shelters, boat ramps for anglers, showers, a dump station, and even a bait shop. There are plenty of nature trails here if you're interested in hiking, and Lake Livingston itself offers some of the best bass fishing in the state.

Spanning the Waters.
Spanning one arm of Lake Livingston, this bridge leads motorists toward Lake Livingston State Park.

Alabama-Coushatta Indian Reservation

The Alabama-Coushatta Indian Reservation was presented to the local Indians by Sam Houston in 1854. The gift was a reward for the tribe's neutral position during the Mexican War of Independence. The main "Indian Village" lies fifteen miles east of Livingston just off US 190 on Park Road 56. It is well marked by signs.

If you pass through the reservation during the spring, summer, or fall, you'll find plenty to occupy your time in the Indian Village, which is open March through October. Indian craftsmen give live arrowmaking and basket-weaving demonstrations throughout the day, and there's also a museum, gift shop, train rides, and a fish-stocked lake. The reservation boasts a large RV campground with all facilities as well, so you can stay a few days if you wish.

I spent several hours here, and the one thing I did not like about the reservation is the attitude of the Indian people toward their guests. There are large signs everywhere telling visitors what they *cannot* do. And quite often, residents are sullen and uncooperative, answering questions that deserve more explanation than monosyllables. The Alabama-Coushatta reservation certainly should not be bypassed, but a few words of warning: Don't expect it to be the friendliest place you've ever encountered.

The Big Thicket

At the town of Woodville, I left US 190 and turned south onto US 69/287, the principal highway bisecting the Big Thicket.

Officially, the Thicket is a federal nature preserve, consisting of about 85,000 acres of wood and marshland, scattered in twelve different units throughout east Texas. There is a visitor center, located just off US 69/287 near the town of Village Mills. Geologically, the preserve can be divided into four different associations—floodplain forest, flatland, Savannah, and hardwood-pine forest. More than 140 types of trees and shrubs are found here, along with a thousand species of flowering plants, 300 kinds of birds, 50 species of reptiles (including five that are poisonous), and more than 60 types of mammals (according to the government pamphlet).

To the folks who live here, though, the Thicket is far more than just an official designation. It might be called an "upland Everglades," a rugged landscape through which one cannot walk except on road or trail because of dense forest and water-filled valley. It might also be called a way of life, a treatise in survival, a monument to nature's everlasting ability to confuse, astonish, and mystify. There are ghost roads here, and "other world" lights, and strange tales of nude hermits, escaped mental patients, and outlaws. And because the Thicket is so remote, its people and their ideas have changed very little in the past two centuries. Outsiders are welcome to visit, poke, and ponder, but they are not accepted; new ideas that vary from the traditional are simply ignored; progress, except in its very mildest form, is seen as the pariah of mankind.

Still as a Statue.
Perched on his private log, a young great blue heron examines his surroundings with a wary eye.

Kirby Nature Trail.
Hikers who utilize this forest pathway will quickly learn how the Big Thicket received its name.

Kirby Nature Trail

My first stop in the "official" Big Thicket was at the visitor center on FM 420. Here, three miles east of US 69/287, there is a small rustic log cabin, a rail fence, and a single park ranger who is probably the loneliest individual in the National Park Service. He didn't have much to say when I arrived except that traffic was light that day (I hadn't seen another car in two hours), and parking my thirty-three-foot-long RV in the small but adequate parking lot out front would cause absolutely no problems.

Exact figures are vague, but according to the brochures that I picked up at the visitor center, the preserve offers about 22 miles of nature trails and 150 miles of backpacking and canoe trails for exploration. One of the shorter paths is the Kirby Nature Trail, a 2-mile-long loop that heads north from the ranger station. Before starting out, I was told by the ranger not to leave the trail for any reason. "If the snakes and 'gators don't get you," he mentioned in passing, "then the forest damn well will."

I left the station about noon, following the twisty, leaf-covered pathway down a hillside through heavy thickets of pine, maple, and gum. Northern cardinals flashed like animated rubies through the trees in front of me; large hawks fluttered overhead, searching for movement and consequently dinner in the forest below. Near a weed-choked stream I spotted several pure-white egrets perched like marble statues in the limbs of a moss-covered tree. Except for the twittering of the songbirds, the wooded landscape was as silent as a grave.

Then, as I moved slowly along the deserted trail, I heard quite a loud rustling of leaves in front of me. Thinking it was probably a deer, I crept ahead, camera at the ready. The noise continued, an ominous CRUMP! CRUMP!, as though Jack's infamous giant had come strolling in the woods. I suddenly asked myself why I was moving *toward* the sound instead of away from it. Visions of angry bears and hungry panthers—both of which inhabit the Thicket—flickered through my mind. CRUMP! CRUMP! The noise was no more than eight or ten yards away, yet still I saw nothing.

Frank "bring 'em back alive" Buck, I'm not. Just as I was about to turn tail and flee, I saw the dead leaves beneath a maple tree fly magically into the air. CRUMP! And there it was. Fangs flashing, standing a full six inches high at the shoulder, the armadillo swallowed the grub it had been chewing, put its nose in the leaves, and pushed with its hind legs. CRUMP! The armor-plated critter moved two feet forward. Not until it was three yards away did it notice me—mouth open—watching. WHANG! It gave one frantic leap straight up, swiveled in mid-air, then bounced away through the trees like a giant mouse. So much for the monster of the Thicket.

Thicket Inhabitant.
An egret stands quietly at the edge of a pond in the Big Thicket, waiting patiently for whatever tender morsel might pass by.

Camping in the Big Thicket

There are no official campgrounds in the preserve, but you'll find three private recreation areas just outside the boundaries. The Big Thicket Campground is located one-half mile east of US 69/287, for instance, on the park entrance road. RV sites are also available at the Big Thicket Outpost just south of Village Mills on US 69/287, and at the Big Thicket RV Park & Campground, located on FM 1003 near the town of Honey Island. Probably the best times to visit are the last of October and early November when the hardwoods change color, and during late April and early May when carpets of legendary Texas wildflowers virtually blanket the forest floor.

Ghost Road

I spent two pleasant days in the Thicket, hiking the quiet nature trails and absorbing the Ozark-Mountainlike atmosphere and culture. Among the towns I recommend for further exploration are Kountze, Honey Island, Village Mills, and Saratoga, all within a short drive of the visitor center and all dependent upon the forest in one way or another for their livelihoods.

Saratoga, for example, once the site of a major oil boom, today depends on tourism. Here you'll find the Big Thicket Museum with its collection of frontier relics, as well as the Bragg "Ghost" Road and its infamous Saratoga Light. The former, a narrow, sandy track that leaves FM 787 just north of town and angles northeast for seven miles through thick loblolly pine, was at one time the bed of the Santa Fe Railroad. The Saratoga Light, a mysterious glow seen only on the darkest nights, is one of those unexplained phenomena that can make even the most meticulous researchers scratch their heads in bewilderment.

The light has been seen on and off for more than fifty years. One theory says it is the lantern of a turn-of-the-century railroad worker who was decapitated by his own train. Another claims it is ghostly flame from a murderous forest fire that once swept through the region. Still another says the light belongs to the ghost of a hunter who was lost in the forest many years ago. (He still wanders, claims the legend, searching for a way out.) And one popular belief states that the light is the ghostly aura of Mexican railroad laborors who were killed by their paycheck-stealing foreman.

Whatever legend one believes, the Saratoga Light is famous, at least in East Texas. It has variously been described as red, white, green, blue, and all sorts of combinations. It has been said to dance, to remain motionless, to dart, leap, and hover. Hundreds, perhaps thousands, of people have seen the light, and it has even been photographed by a well-known *National Geographic* photographer.

Visiting the Light

My own experience with the Saratoga Light nearly scared me out of ten years' growth. I had spent the afternoon in the Big Thicket Museum, then in late afternoon turned the nose of my rig north toward the Woodsy Hollow Campground just south of Goodrich. Situated on the edge of a small forest lake, this thirty-acre campground is one of the prettiest and best-equipped RV parks in Texas. I was hooked up by 7 P.M. and had just finished the supper dishes when Gordon Packy, my next-door neighbor, arrived, smile on his face, eyes gleaming.

Gordon is a retired university professor from Austin who has been coming to the Thicket each fall and winter for about five years. Did I want to go see the Saratoga Light that very evening? Not particularly, since I'm less than fond of spooky occurrences. Nonetheless, I loaded my cameras into his small tag-along, and we set out, arriving at the junction of FM 787 and the Bragg Road about an hour later. Gordon drove a mile or so up the rutty track, parked in a wide spot, and killed the lights and engine. Outside, the moonless night was black as pitch.

Gordon suggested I set up my camera and tripod just in front of the car. "You know," he said when I returned, "this place gives rise to more strange stories than any other part of Texas. Some folks swear there are still outlaws living in the woods. Guess you've heard about that naked fellow—the one with the guns?"

I said I hadn't, didn't necessarily want to, and would he please shut up, but Gordon's tongue wagged on. "Around here, he's known as the 'Nude

Ghost Light.
Barely discernible in the distance, the Saratoga Light is thought to be the ghost of a decapitated railroad man in search of his head.

Man of the Big Thicket.' A hermit, the story goes, big, strong, and hairy, with a long gray beard, carries a gun in each hand when he's out wandering. He hasn't hurt anyone yet but there are lots of unexplained disappearances in these woods."

I rolled up my window and locked my door. Gordon chattered away, relating every detail of every Thicket legend he could remember, including the life history of the infamous railroad engineer without a head. When the Saratoga Light suddenly appeared down the road two hours later, I was so intimidated by thoughts of untidy Thicket Thingies I didn't want to get out of the car.

I finally slipped out the door and crept around the fender to push the shutter release on my camera. The light, a steady yellowish glow four or five hundred feet down the road, didn't seem to be getting closer, so I chanced half a dozen exposures before throwing my gear into the back seat. Turning down Gordon's offer to move us closer, I again locked my door and pointed toward home. We arrived back at Woodsy Hollow about midnight and I made sure my door was securely locked before climbing into bed.

Sleepy Hollow Lake.
Sleepy Hollow Lake, situated in the Big Thicket area south of Goodrich, offers both serene views and recreational opportunities among piney woods.

Side Trip to Galveston

The traffic in Houston is absolutely the worst in Texas, but if you don't mind congestion and smog I recommend taking a short side trip to the resort city of Galveston. Located on the Gulf Coast about sixty miles south of Houston, this historic seaport is well worth the drive down from the Thicket. To get there take US 59 south to I-45, then follow the interstate southeast to the Galveston Causeway.

Before a hurricane literally wiped it off the map in 1900, Galveston was the pride and joy of the Lone Star State. The largest and wealthiest port of the Gulf of Mexico west of New Orleans, its streets were lined with Victorian mansions, and sailing ships from the world's seven oceans arrived and departed daily. The gold and glitter disappeared, however, when a massive storm virtually flattened Galveston, killing 5,000 people in the process and sinking scores of ships.

Today, the thirty-mile-long barrier island on which Galveston sits is a haven for RVers. Here you'll find miles of white sand beach, phenomenal deep-sea fishing, a fine historical museum, an automobile museum, the family-oriented Sea-Arama Marineworld, and a beautiful downtown historic district. If you want to spend a few days exploring, I suggest staying at Galveston Island State Park, six miles south of the city on FM 3005. Located directly on the beach, the park has shelters, restrooms, showers, dump stations, and of course, all hookups.

The Elissa

One of Galveston's "don't miss" attractions is the square-rigged sailing ship *Elissa.* Built in Aberdeen, Scotland, in 1877, the ship spent the first four decades of her life on the high seas, hauling lumber, cotton, and coal from one exotic port of call to another. At the end of World War I, however, her sailing days abruptly came to an end when, unable to compete with faster steam-powered ships, she was "hauled" in Sweden and equipped with an engine. Her three tall but useless masts were removed and the graceful sailing bow replaced with the blunt snout of a coastal freighter. For the next forty years she clanked and groaned through the Mediterranean—a decrepit tramp steamer barely able to earn her keep. Then in the mid-1970s, after a short career smuggling cigarettes from Yugoslavia to Italy, the *Elissa* was sent to Piraeus, Greece, scheduled to be scrapped once and for all.

Meanwhile, as part of a city-wide restoration project designed to once again make Galveston a popular tourist resort, a search had begun for a square-rigged sailing ship that could be used as a downtown nautical museum. City officials located the *Elissa* in Greece and purchased the old ship only days before she was to be destroyed. Two years later she arrived in Galveston, where the local historical foundation set about the long and difficult task of restoration.

Over the next thirty-five months, the *Elissa* underwent a complete facelift. Her hull was replated, her engine removed, the bilges were

Tall Ship in the Harbor.
One of the best-kept square-rigged sailing ships on earth, and one of Galveston's most popular attractions, the *Elissa* heads for the open gulf off Galveston Island. A hundred years ago, similar ships left Galveston Harbor on a daily basis for all the ports of the world.

cleaned, all decks were replaced, and new masts and yardarms were cut and installed. Sailmakers were commissioned to replace the 12,000 square feet of canvas she had originally carried, and thousands of yards of new lines and rigging were patiently spliced into place. Galveston businessmen, eager to help, donated not only hard cash, but tons of material and equipment as well. Local residents by the hundreds pitched in on weekends, anxious to assist wherever they could.

On July 4, 1982, *Elissa's* gangplank was lowered and she was opened to the public. The restoration cost was $4 million and 20,000 hours of

Feathered Beachcombers.
Shorebirds by the hundreds are common sights along the miles of Galveston's white-sand beaches.

human labor, but within a year more than 100,000 visitors had toured the vessel, making her one of the most successful nautical museums in America. Today you can explore the old ship any day of the week at Pier 21 in downtown Galveston (there's a small admission charge). And for a true visual feast, visit the city in late October when the *Elissa* sets all 12,000 square feet of canvas and gracefully sails up and down Galveston Bay. Only crew members are allowed on board during these sea trials, but the photographs you'll get of the ship under way will be magnificent.

Back to the Primeval

Once your visit to Galveston is over, I suggest you return to the Big Thicket on US 59; it's the quickest and most scenic route available. I returned to the town of Cleveland, then joined FM 1725 west, which carried me back into the Sam Houston National Forest and finally to Huntsville. My Big Thicket odyssey ended where it had begun, beneath the quiet canopy of hardwoods in Huntsville State Park. There I spent another day exploring that sanctuary's lovely nature trails before heading north toward other adventures.

POINTS OF INTEREST: Texas Tour 6

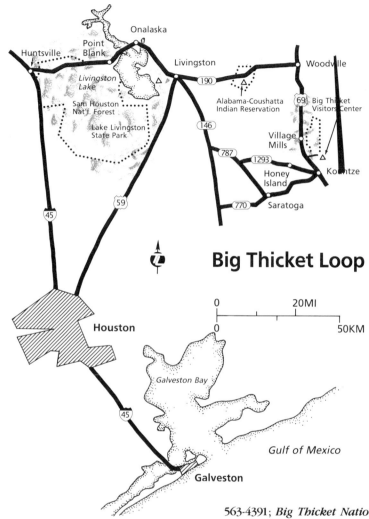

Big Thicket Loop

0   20MI

0   50KM

ACCESS: *I-45* north from Houston to Huntsville; *US 190* east to Woodville; *US 69/287* south to the Big Thicket.

INFORMATION: *Huntsville Chamber of Commerce,* PO Box 538, Huntsville, TX 77340, (409) 295-8113; *Huntsville State Park,* PO Box 508, Huntsville, TX 77340, (409) 295-5644; *Polk County-Livingston Chamber of Commerce,* 516 W. Church, Livingston, TX 77351, (409) 327-4929; *Alabama-Coushatta Indian Reservation,* Route 3, Box 640, Livingston, TX 77351, (409)

563-4391; *Big Thicket National Preserve,* 8185 Eastex Freeway, Beaumont, TX 77708, (409) 839-2689; *Galveston Convention & Visitors Bureau,* 2106 Seawall Blvd., Galveston, TX 77550, (800) 351-4237.

ANNUAL EVENTS:

Galveston: *Mardi Gras* (street dancing, parades), February; *Dickens Festival* (various Christmas celebrations), December.

MUSEUMS & GALLERIES:

Huntsville: *Sam Houston Museum,* 1804 Sam Houston Ave., Tuesday–Sunday, 9 A.M.–5 P.M., 19th-century pioneer artifacts.

Livingston: *Polk County Museum,* 601 West Church St., Monday–Friday, 1–5 P.M., Indian, pioneer artifacts.

Saratoga: *Big Thicket Museum,* Highway 770, Tuesday–Saturday, 9 A.M.–5 P.M., Sunday, 1 P.M.–5 P.M., Big Thicket artifacts, relics.

Galveston: *Automobile Museum,* 23rd and Avenue M, 10 A.M.–5 P.M. daily, various antique autos; *Galveston Historical Museum,* 2219 Market St., Monday–Friday, 9 A.M.–4 P.M., Saturday, 11 A.M.–4 P.M., early Galveston artifacts; *Sea-Arama Marineworld,* Seawall Blvd. at 91st St. 10 A.M. till dark daily, marine showcase, trained animals.

RESTAURANTS:

Huntsville: *Junction Steak & Seafood,* 11th St., 3 blocks off I-45, American family-style dining.

Point Blank: *Miss Emily's,* Highway US 190, family-style dining.

Livingston: *Golden Corral,* US 190, west end of town, steak and seafood.

Galveston: *Gaidos,* 39th and Seawall Blvd., seafood.

Northeast Texas

Sabrina Fair,
   Listen where thou art sitting
Under the glassy, cool, translucent
      wave,
      In twisted braids of lilies knitting
The loose train of thy amber-dropping
      hair;
      Listen for dear honor's sake
      Goddess of the silver lake,
         Listen and save.

John Milton,
Comus, 1634

The Brazos River begins in the northwest corner of Texas and ends when its muddy contents mingle with the sparkling, emerald-green waters of the Gulf of Mexico near the coastal town of Freeport. A thousand miles in length, it is the third longest river in Texas.

I didn't explore the Brazos from end to end, though an RV tour through the entire Brazos River Valley, from Lubbock to Freeport for example, would certainly be interesting. Instead, I joined the waterway near the community of Marlin and followed it northwest through the breathtaking Texas Lake District to Possum Kingdom State Park, west of Fort Worth. I'll warn you that visitor attractions, other than water-related activities like fishing and boating, aren't numerous in this isolated rural landscape, but if you just want to ramble, enjoy the countryside, and meet the local folks, there is no better place in the state.

Tour 7 *308 miles*
Side Trip to Fort Worth, 48 miles

MARLIN • BRAZOS COUNTY PARK •
WACO • LAKE WHITNEY • CLIFTON •
DINOSAUR VALLEY STATE PARK •
GRANBURY • LAKE MINERAL WELLS
STATE PARK • FORT WORTH •
POSSUM KINGDOM LAKE

Marlin

According to local fishermen, Marlin, Texas, is a quiet little town most of the time, changing pace only on summer weekends when thousands of funseekers arrive from nearby Waco, searching for a bit of cool Brazos River water in which to soak their feet or drown a worm. Established in 1830 by settlers who spent more time fighting Indians than they did clearing and farming the land, it remained little more than a frontier outpost until the 1890s. Then, when drillers struck hot artesian waters just a few feet below the earth's surface, Marlin suddenly boomed. "Miracle waters!" town fathers shouted from the rooftops, and the ill and infirm came by the thousands. The boom has long since busted, but the artesian wells still pump faithfully, providing heat for several of the town's municipal buildings. About the only visitor attractions here are a small county museum and a nineteenth-century manor house, Highlands Mansion.

Brazos County Park

There is but one traveler's park in the vicinity of Marlin, Brazos County Park, a small, county-operated fishermen's campground eight miles southwest of town on FM 712. Situated just a few yards from the banks of the Brazos River, the place is a bit buggy on warm evenings, but nonetheless a pleasant, cool, and friendly RV sanctuary.

If you like to fish, the 300-yard-long Brazos River pool just below the campground has a reputation for producing large catfish. The day before I arrived, two yellow cats (known also as "flatheads") weighing fifty pounds apiece were caught on rod and reel by a local angler within sight of the park. The river also contains black bass, white bass, and perch.

Birdlife on the river is profuse. Flocks of shore and wading birds feed fearlessly in the shallows, while ducks of every size and description quack

Backlit Beauty.
Fresh to the world, a leggy Arabian colt surveys his surroundings near the Brazos River.

and gurgle in deeper water. Waiting for a steak to cook on my charcoal grill one evening, I watched a trio of great egrets attend to their courting ritual less than twenty yards from my campsite. For long moments the graceful birds stood facing each other like marble statues; then one opened his wings and danced—up and down, back and forth, like a slender puppet on a string. After a minute or so, he froze, then danced again, then froze again. Finally, some secret rite known only to egrets was accomplished, and the birds went about their separate ways, searching for fish and grubs in the riverside mud.

Six-Shooter Junction

After a night at the park and an hour the next morning exploring the county museum's collection of frontier memorabilia, I headed west from Marlin on SR 6 toward Waco.

Founded in 1837 by the Texas Rangers, this small, horizontal metropolis, known as the "City of Five Cs" (cotton, cattle, corn, collegians, and

Still Standing.
In a field just south of Lake Whitney, this ancient roadside building could have been constructed in Civil War days.

culture), has seen many changes during its long and colorful past. Before the Civil War, for instance, Waco was famous throughout the south for its sprawling and highly prosperous cotton plantations and sophisticated, high-living society. As the war progressed and northern troops moved south, however, the plantations were razed and their owners either killed or scattered. Later in history the town boomed again, this time as "Six-shooter Junction," a wild, lawless community on the Chisholm cattle trail, where hell-raising cowboys found solace in the arms of prostitutes, where shootings were commonplace, and where saloons outnumbered churches fifty to one.

Today the home of Baylor University and three smaller colleges, Waco is an educated, cultural town, appreciated for its beauty, good taste, and quiet simplicity by visitors and locals alike. If you decide to drive in for a morning, make your first stop the Texas Ranger Hall of Fame, located just off I-35 on the shores of Lake Brazos. Housed in a replica of Fort Fisher (the original Texas Ranger fort built in 1837), the museum displays a famous collection of old-west firearms, Indian artifacts, western art, and plenty of relics and memorabilia from the Texas Rangers themselves. Among the city's other "must-sees" are the well-known Strecker Museum, the Cen-Tex zoo, and the half-dozen gracious antebellum mansions in the historic district that were not destroyed in the Civil War. If you need more than a day, RV camping is available at Lake Brazos near the Texas Ranger Hall of Fame. A thirty-five-acre park adjacent to the museum along the Brazos River offers all hookups and plenty of privacy.

Lake Whitney

North of Waco along FM 933, the landscape is radically different from the heavily timbered terrain of the Big Thicket region just a few miles to the south and east. Corn, cotton, and alfalfa fields have replaced the trees and lie on the softly rolling hills like a multicolored chessboard. Vine-covered hedgerows separate the fields and small farms; barns and houses are old and weathered, many of them constructed before the Civil War. The countryside is very "English" in appearance. I've seen similar landscapes in the Lake District north of London, in North Wales, and even in New Zealand.

At the junction of FM 933 and FM 2114, I turned west on the latter toward Lake Whitney, and when the skies opened up twenty minutes later, I decided to call it a day. Half a mile past the Whitney Lake Dam Bridge on SR 22, I pulled into Lofers Bend Park, paid my fee, and headed for shelter.

Lake Whitney is an outdoor lover's paradise, rain or shine. Snakelike in shape, this 24,000-acre Corps of Engineers reservoir is one of the finest warm-water fishing lakes in Texas, containing black and white bass, perch, and catfish. Scuba diving in the extremely clear water is also popular, as is boating, water-skiing, and sailing. Scattered around the lakeshore are five large travelers' parks, which offer complete motorhome and travel-trailer

A Most Graceful Bird.
Egrets, like this one on the Brazos River near Marlin, are among the world's most beautiful and graceful birds.

Lofers Bend Park.
One of five large travelers' parks scattered around Lake Whitney, Lofers Bend is blanketed with wildflowers in the spring.

accommodations. Lofers Bend, Lake Whitney State Park, McCown Valley Park, and Cedar Creek Park are located on the southeast shore, while Cedron Creek Park is on the southwest.

Lofers Bend is typical of the lake's campgrounds and recreation areas. The park is huge and for the most part open, offering campers in almost all areas beautiful views of the lake. There are more than a hundred sites here, many of them on the lakeshore itself and none more than a five-minute walk from the water. The vast majority of the terrain is covered in grass, and all roads in the park are paved. And at all the parks on Whitney, volunteers at the main gate will give you a sheet of paper, containing not only the park rules and regulations, but also telephone numbers of the local sheriff, hospital, and parks and wildlife department. Folks here really seem to care whether or not you are comfortable.

Clifton

From Lake Whitney I recommend taking SR 22 west to its junction with FM 219, then heading southwest to the town of Clifton. About six miles from the turnoff, start watching to the right for the Clifton Rooster Ranch. Perhaps a hundred of these finely feathered fowl are tethered in front of their fifty-five-gallon-drum homes like dogs. I'm not sure visitors are welcome to just browse, but the owner doesn't mind if you stand near the highway and take pictures. The rabble of roosters is quite a sight, strutting around on their leashes. You might think it would be a miserable existence, living next to the ranch, but the owner told me he had trained the roosters to crow only at dawn and not a moment before.

Almost Pettable.
Silhouetted against the dark forest of Texas Safari Wildlife Park, this young deer seems tame enough to pet.

The community of Clifton was settled in 1854 and has the distinction of being the largest Norwegian settlement in Texas. Its primary attraction, however, is neither sardines nor saunas but the Texas Safari Wildlife Park. Roaming free on 850 acres of Africanlike veld and forest are more than forty different species of exotic animals, including the rare white rhino, cape buffalo, and zebra.

Once you've paid your entry fee at the main gate, you're free to drive the single paved road through the sanctuary at your leisure (the speed limit is five miles per hour). You can't leave your vehicle, but there's plenty to see out the windows. You'll seldom need even a telephoto lens on your camera to photograph the resident critters, in fact. The park is open seven days a week from 10 A.M. until an hour before sundown.

Walking Tank.
A white rhino, one of the larger inhabitants of the Texas Safari Wildlife Park, shows off its armament.

On the Trail of the Dinosaurs

My next stop was the town of Glen Rose where I followed US 67 west and then a short park road to Dinosaur Valley State Park. Located on the Paluxy River four miles from town, the park consists of 1,500 scrub-covered acres in the rolling limestone hills of the Brazos River Valley. There's plenty of RV camping available if you want to spend a few days exploring the region.

Petrified Past.
Preserved in the hardened mud of the Paluxy River, this huge dinosaur track was probably made by *Acrocanthosaurus,* a 30-foot-long relative of *Tyrannosaurus rex.*

The park's principal attractions are its dinosaur tracks, most of them frozen forever in the hardened mud of the Paluxy River bottom. Most common are three-toed, birdlike imprints of the *Acrocanthosaurus,* a thirty-foot-long relative of the legendary *Tyrannosaurus rex.* Another common track is a three-foot-long saucerlike depression belonging to *Pleurocoelus,* a plant-eating sauropod with a serpentine neck and pillarlike legs. There's a third type of track in the park as well, one made by a mysterious three-toed reptile that has yet to be identified. Many scientists think it may belong to an *Iguanodon,* a giant lizard previously thought to have lived only in Europe.

Scientists have learned much from studying the tracks in Dinosaur Valley State Park. By the length of its stride, for instance, they've learned that *Acrocanthosaurus* traveled about five miles an hour when chasing down a *Pleurocoelus,* which could struggle along at only $2^{7}/_{10}$ miles an hour. They also now know that sauropods were herd animals, moving from bog to bog in groups of some two dozen individuals. You'll enjoy poking around the exhibits here, even if you don't care how fast a dinosaur could do the hundred-yard dash. Some of the hiking trails are a bit rugged, but most are short and interesting. The park also has an excellent museum that offers an in-depth look at dinosaur development in North America.

Granbury

If there is a friendlier or livelier town in Texas than Granbury, I haven't been there. Located about twenty miles north of Glen Rose on SR 144, the small community of 5,000 people also has lots of unique attractions for

Civil War Relived.
Soldiers march off to battle in a reenactment of a Civil War skirmish during General Granbury's Birthday Party and Bean Cookoff, held each year in Granbury.

visitors. Across the street from the historic and beautiful Hood County Courthouse, for instance, be sure to visit the Granbury Opera House, originally constructed in 1886 and restored to its old-west splendor in 1975. Plays, musicals, and melodramas are presented by a local acting group from March to December several times each day. I had the chance to attend one of these mini-theatricals, and it is well worth the small price of admission. Another popular attraction is the *Granbury Queen,* a seventy-three-foot-long replica of a pre-Civil War paddle-wheel riverboat. From March through October she carries passengers on daily sightseeing cruises of nearby Lake Granbury and the Brazos River Valley. And if you happen to visit on the second Saturday in March, attend General Granbury's Birthday Party and Bean Cookoff, held in the historic square adjacent to the Hood County Courthouse. This day-long celebration features parades, all sorts of arts and crafts booths, and more food than you could eat in a month of Sundays. It's Granbury's big event of the year, so don't pass it by.

Brazos River Rattlesnake Ranch

Why any normal human being would want to visit a rattlesnake ranch is beyond me, but I went anyway (even though my better judgment kept shouting "stupid!"). The place sits northwest of Granbury, just past the junction of US 281 and I-20 and is well marked by signs.

The Brazos River Rattlesnake Ranch is owned by Bob and Phyllus Popplewell. Bob is a retired sociologist who decided he wanted to do something that was more fun than dealing with worldly problems. Today he spends most of his time trapping vagrant reptiles out of neighbors' yards. Phyllus told me her husband had been bitten several times in the past few years but never—at least not that she could determine—fatally.

The place is actually kind of fun. Outside, there's a large open pit that contains more than 250 live Texas diamondback rattlers, plus another area where you can see water moccasins, copperheads, and several species of nonvenomous snakes. Inside, there are tables filled with freeze-dried and stuffed rattlers of all shapes and sizes. The ranch also sells watchbands, hatbands, jewelry, and similar paraphernalia, all made of snakeskin. Visitors are welcome to browse but shouldn't stick their fingers into any dark corners.

Lake Mineral Wells State Park

Leaving the rattlesnakes to those with plenty of visceral puissance (courage), I followed US 281 northwest to Mineral Wells, then turned east on US 180 to Lake Mineral Wells State Park, five miles out of town. Another of those peaceful, hiking-fishing-birdwatching parks so carefully groomed for visitors by the state of Texas, the 2,800 acres of woodlands and water here are popular with RVers and day-users from the entire central and north Texas region.

Who Says Snakes Aren't Cute?
Phyllus Popplewell, from the Brazos River Rattlesnake Ranch, carefully holds a five-foot rattler. Actually the scaly fellow was stuffed by Phyllus's husband, Bob.

Alert Gander.
A Canada goose, visiting Lake Mineral Wells State Park to feed and rest, takes time out from stuffing itself on seeds and grass to pose for a photograph.

There are three major campgrounds with a total of seventy-seven RV sites in the park, all located on the northwest shore of the lake. Each site has water and electricity but no sewer. You'll find a dump station, however, near the visitor center. Park facilities include a number of maintained hiking and nature trails, rental canoes, and a small store. Boaters can use the bass-filled lake, but there's a fifteen-mile-per-hour speed limit because of swimmers.

Side Trip to Fort Worth

There's not much to see in the town of Mineral Wells, so if you want to go exploring, head for nearby Fort Worth, an hour's drive to the east on US 180. Though it's near Dallas and by association often included in the "Big D's" smoggy, congested, and traffic-heavy metro-complex, Fort Worth resembles its nearby big brother not at all.

Founded in 1849 as a military outpost and appropriately nicknamed "cow-town," Fort Worth is basically a small, neighborly community that suddenly found itself with 400,000 residents. For RVers, it's an easy city to get around in. Well-marked attractions, wide streets, and light traffic even during rush hours make it almost pleasant to negotiate, even in large motorhomes.

Make your first cow-town stop the Stockyards, a newly renovated area of western-wear and curio shops, galleries, and good restaurants on the north side of town. The place is fun to visit. Mounted cowboys ride the streets, and residents and shopkeepers often wear circa-1880 costumes. There's a bar here that boasts saddles for stools, and even a photography

Rising High in Fort Worth.
Though known by its residents as "Cow Town," Fort Worth is actually an ultra-modern city of 400,000. A downtown skyscraper is but one of many which make up the community's dramatic skyline.

Downtown Murals.
Depicting a time gone by, these huge murals of an 1870 cattle drive on the side of a downtown Fort Worth building have helped to establish the city's nickname of "Cow Town."

Prehistoric to Picasso.
The Kimbell Art Museum in Fort Worth is one of the world's most famous show-cases for paintings and sculpture.

studio in which you can dress up in outlaw clothing for a family portrait. If you need a new pair of western boots, a ten-gallon hat, or a silver-inlay saddle, this is the place. Competition among western-wear stores is ferocious so prices are quite low.

I heartily recommend visiting two of Fort Worth's many museums. First is the Kimbell Art Museum, an ultra-modern "cycloid-vault" structure on Camp Bowie Boulevard whose theme is "Prehistoric to Picasso." The other, just a few blocks up the street is the Amon G. Carter Museum of Western Art. The permanent collection of works by Fredric Remington and Charles Russell on display here is among the best in the world.

Other things you might want to see are the lovely Japanese Garden in Trinity Park, the highly acclaimed Science and History Museum on Montgomery Street, and Log Cabin Village in Forest Park. Downtown, stop at the amazing Water Garden, a spectacular public park filled with cascading fountains, adjacent to the convention center. Also downtown is Sundance Square, named naturally for the legendary Sundance Kid (who, along with Butch Cassidy, once hid out here). Another city renovation project, the square offers an entire block of galleries and souvenir shops to explore. A favorite attraction here are the Clydesdale-pulled carriages that carry sightseers on short tours of the downtown area.

Trinity Park.
Visitors meander through the beautiful Japanese Garden in Fort Worth's famed Trinity Park.

Kingdom of the Possums

I topped off my tour of the lake district with a stay at Possum Kingdom Lake State Recreation Area, fifty-five road miles (shorter as the crow flies) west of Mineral Wells. To get there I drove west on US 180 to the tiny

Evening Mist.
Silhouetted against Possum Kingdom Lake, a camper observes one of the prettiest sights in Texas—mist rising from the water like cream-colored smoke.

farm town of Caddo, then turned north onto Park Road 33. The park lies seventeen miles from the junction.

I heard about the lake from a number of RVers, virtually all of them agreeing that it was one of the prettiest impoundments in Texas. Located in the rugged canyon country of the Palo Pinto Mountains, the lake encompasses 20,000 acres of the clearest, bluest water in the American Southwest. In the adjacent traveler's park, fifty-eight RV and tent sites are available, most of them with water and electricity. There's also a small gas and grocery store, a boat-launching ramp, and a 300-foot-long lighted fishing pier for night angling.

My best memories are from the first evening I spent at the park. I arrived in late afternoon. The air was cooling rapidly and a light mist arose from the water, hovering like cream-colored smoke a few feet above the surface. Wild ducks played noisily along the bank and an osprey flickered by overhead, a fish clutched firmly in its claws. In the brush near my campsite, a young white-tailed buck browsed unhurriedly, totally fearless of my presence, even when I climbed out of my RV's cab to hook up. The whole scene could have been straight out of the pages of J. J. R. Tolkien's *Lord of the Rings*. Frankly, I wouldn't have been a bit surprised to see a woolly-pated hobbit accompanied by a family of elves go prancing by on their way to the Misty Mountains.

POINTS OF INTEREST: Texas Tour 7

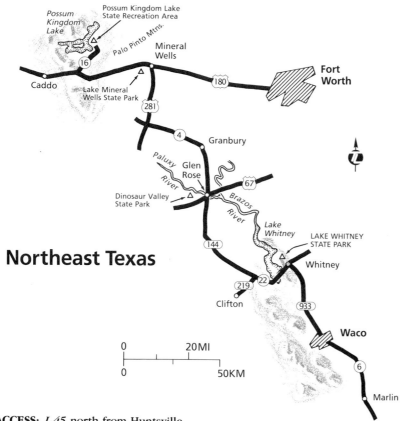

Northeast Texas

ACCESS: *I-45 north from Huntsville.*

INFORMATION: *Marlin Chamber of Commerce,* P.O. Box 369, Marlin, TX 76661, (817) 883-2171; *Waco Visitor Information Center,* University Park Dr. off I-35, Waco, TX 76702, (817) 753-1505; *Whitney Lake Area,* Whitney Project Office, P.O. Box 38, Laguna Park, TX 76634, (817) 694-3189; *Texas Safari Wildlife Park,* Route 2, Clifton, TX 76634, (817) 675-3658; *Dinosaur Valley State Park,* P.O. Box 396, Glen Rose, TX 76043, (817) 897-4588; *Granbury Chamber of Commerce,* P.O. Box 277, Granbury, TX 76048, (817) 573-1622; *Lake Mineral Wells State Park,* Route 4, Box 39C, Mineral Wells, TX 76067, (817) 328-1171; *Fort Worth Convention & Visitors Bureau,* 100 East 15th St., #400, Fort Worth, TX 76102, (817) 336-8791; *Possum Kingdom State Recreation Area,* Box 36, Caddo, TX 76029, (817) 549-1803.

ANNUAL EVENTS:

Waco: *Brazos River Festival* (arts and crafts and tours), third week in April; *Heart O' Texas Fair & Rodeo* (professional rodeo, carnival, fine arts exhibit), first week in October; *Christmas-on-the-Brazos,* first weekend in December.

Granbury: *General Granbury's Birthday Party & Bean Cookoff* (parades, food booths), second Saturday in March.

Fort Worth: *Fat Stock Show & Rodeo,* late January and early February; *Colonial Golf Classic,* May; *Chisholm Trail Roundup* (cowboy events, parades), second weekend in June; *Pioneer Days* (parades, arts and crafts, street exhibitions), last weekend in September.

MUSEUMS & GALLERIES:

Marlin: *Falls County Museum,* 141 Railroad St., Monday, Tuesday, 10 A.M.–4 P.M., Wednesday–Friday, 1 P.M.–4 P.M., Saturday and Sunday, 2 P.M.–5 P.M., historical exhibits.

Waco: *Texas Ranger Hall of Fame & Museum,* I-35 at Riverside Drive, June–August, 9 A.M.–6 P.M. daily, September–April, 9 A.M.–5 P.M. daily, old-west exhibits, western art: *Strecker Museum,* Baylor University Campus, Monday–Friday, 9 A.M.–4 P.M. Saturday, 2 P.M.–5 P.M., historical, anthropological exhibits.

Clifton: *Bosque Memorial Museum,* South Avenue Q and West 9th, Friday, Saturday, Sunday, 10 A.M.–5 P.M., geologic, historical exhibits.

Granbury: *Hood County Jail,* 208 North Crockett, Monday–Friday 9 A.M.–5 P.M., original cell blocks, hanging tower.

Fort Worth: *Amon G. Carter Museum of Western Art,* 3501 Camp Bowie Boulevard, Tuesday–Saturday, 10 A.M.–5 P.M., Sunday, 1:30 A.M.–5 P.M., western paintings, sculptures, photographs; *Kimbell Art Museum,* 3333 Camp Bowie Blvd., Tuesday–Saturday, 10 A.M.–5 P.M., Sunday, 11 A.M.–5 P.M., modern art displays; *Museum Of Science & History,* 1501 Montgomery St., Monday–Saturday, 9 A.M.–5 P.M., Sunday, 2 P.M.–5 P.M., science and history exhibits.

RESTAURANTS:

Granbury: *Cuckoo's Nest,* Pearl St. (near the courthouse), home-style cooking; *Nutthouse,* 121 East Bridge St., home-style cooking.

Waco: *Tanglewood Farms,* I-35 & Second St. (Fort Fisher exit), family-style dining; *Western Choice Steakhouse,* 200 I-35 West, steak and chicken.

Fort Worth: *Williams Ranch House,* 5532 Jacksboro Hwy, steak & seafood; *Robert's,* 215 University Dr., steak and seafood; *Sardines,* 3410 Camp Bowie Blvd., Italian food.

LAND OF BEYOND
The Panhandle

Have ever you stood where the silences brood,
And vast the horizons begin,
At the dawn of the day to behold far away
The goal you would strive for and win?
Yet ah! in the night when you gain to the height,
With the vast pool of heaven star-spawned,
Afar and agleam, like a valley of dream,
Still mocks you a Land of Beyond.

Robert Service,
The Land of Beyond

The Texas Panhandle does not really look much like the handle of a pan. Nor, for that matter, does the state of Texas resemble the pan itself. Many states, Florida and Oklahoma among them, also boast panhandles, and frankly none of them look like pans. Or pots. Or skillets.

The *Thorndike Barnhart Advanced Dictionary* defines panhandle as "a narrow strip of land projecting like a handle." That doesn't tell us much. A bit farther down, however, their definition of panhandler is "to beg, especially in the streets." Does that mean that all those pleasant folks who reside in the panhandles of Texas, Florida, and Oklahoma—known, naturally, as Panhandlers—are street beggars? I think not. Sometimes words certainly play strange and unusual games with us.

I suppose the Texas Panhandle can best be described as the north-westernmost corner of the state, north of an imaginary line drawn from the city of Kermit on the western border to Wichita Falls on the east. It is basically farm country, thousands of square miles of flatland, low, timber-covered hills, and surprisingly dramatic canyons. Buffalo once roamed here and the deer and antelope still play (if you can find them). It is one of the few places in America where you can stand in the middle of a plowed field and see nothing—not even a telephone pole—but that same plowed field in a 360-degree eye sweep of the horizon.

Tour 8 *330 miles*

WICHITA FALLS • VERNON • QUANAH • COPPER BREAKS STATE PARK • CAPROCK CANYONS STATE PARK • CANYON • AMARILLO • PALO DURO CANYON STATE PARK

Wichita Falls

I started my Panhandle tour in the city of Wichita Falls, named for a waterfall that once existed on the Wichita River but which has long been lost to progress. Why anyone would wish to remove a waterfall from its natural habitat is beyond me. I asked, but nobody knew. There is, however, a re-creation of the falls on I-44, about a mile south of the Texas Tourist Bureau in Wichita Falls that's well worth a stop.

With a population of nearly 100,000, Wichita Falls calls itself a city, but it still displays a neighborly, small-town attitude toward visitors. Residents are downright friendly and will go out of their way to help if you need it. If you feel like exploring the city, there's an excellent museum and art center here, the former with its own planetarium. Nearby Lake Arrowhead State Park (fourteen miles south via US 281) has plenty of RV sites, plus hiking trails and fishing. If you want to be closer in, try the Wichita Falls RV Park, a small, roadside, city-owned park located just off I-44, two blocks south of the Texas Tourist Bureau.

Into the Panhandle

I left Wichita Falls on US 287 heading west, following the Red River along the border of Oklahoma. The most prominent feature of the landscape here is that it doesn't *have* a prominent feature The terrain is simply flat

Vertical Vistas.
The steep cliffs and lovely views at Palo Duro Canyon are among the most breath-taking sights in the American Southwest.

Almost Real.
Though constructed by man, this waterfall in Wichita Falls closely resembles a natural one on the Wichita River that no longer exists.

farm and cattle country, covered with grass, divided by fence, and stretching away as far as the eye can see in all directions.

The earth looks dry, often wasted. When one of the great Panhandle "toad-stranglers" occurs, however, perhaps three or four times each year, things change quickly. Often, too much water rather than too little is the problem, in fact. Usually it happens in late July and August when the big thunderheads roll into the American Southwest from the Pacific. They mass together over the flatlands in flotilla form, and when enough have collected, when enough slivers of lightning have been hurled earthward to appease the gods, it rains. Not a drizzle, not a downpour, but an onslaught—a driving, vertical tidal wave that can deposit 100,000 gallons of moisture on a single square mile of land in five minutes.

It is not until after the rains have passed, however, that the real drama of a "toad-strangler" begins. When the ocher-stained earth of the Red River Valley has absorbed all it can, the water must go elsewhere. It does, quickly filling the depressions and smaller gullies before spilling into the larger ones. The resulting phenomenon, known as a flashflood, is more feared by Panhandlers than is a tornado by a Kansas farm town. To call it "flood" is misleading. Force would be a better description. Anything on the gully floor—rattlesnakes, scorpions, drift logs, boulders, people, automobiles—is caught up on the watery explosion and carried down the normally dry wash at the speed of an Amtrak express. If you happen to be in western Texas during July and August and are planning to camp out, take care where you park your rig.

Vernon

Once known as Eagle Flats because of a large group of eagles that nested nearby, the small town of Vernon (population 13,000) is typical of most farm and ranch communities in the Panhandle. It isn't especially attractive, but to the many rural families in the area it is the hub around which all life exists. There are gasoline stations here, drug stores, markets, farm machinery repairs and sales, the inevitable drive-in restaurant. There is also a sizable oil field here, and in places the terrain is virtually covered with pumping oil wells. "Black Gold" is the lifeblood of Vernon and surrounding communities, and over the years millions of barrels have been slurped from the great reservoir below the earth's surface.

If you want to explore, visit the R. L. More Bird Egg Collection, started in 1888 and presently consisting of 10,000 eggs from more than 750 different species of birds. The collection is housed at 1905 Wilbarger Street, and visitors are welcome. Another of Vernon's attractions is the Red River Valley Museum, featuring archaeological and Indian exhibits from the surrounding area.

Antiques and Wooden Indians

In the town of Quanah, be sure to stop at Terry's Antiques, owned and operated by Jim and Irma Terry. Over the years the Terrys have amassed one of the world's greatest collections of hand-carved, cigar-store wooden Indians. The store is also filled with other antiques, from chamber pots to Victorian furniture. If you need information on the region, this pleasant couple will be happy to supply it.

Quanah itself was named for Quanah Parker, last great war chief of the Comanche and one of the better known Indian figures in western legend. Son of a Comanche chief and a captive white girl, Parker and his small band of warriors probably gave more grief to the United States Army than any other Native American leader in history.

Quanah's mother was Cynthia Ann Parker, one of five captives taken by the Comanche during a raid on Parker's Fort in central Texas in 1836. A few years after the raid, she became the wife of Nokoni, a popular chief in the "wanderer" band of the Comanches. Cynthia had two sons and a daughter by Nokoni. When she was rescued by the Texas Rangers twenty-four years after her capture, she took her daughter with her. Both sons, however, remained with the Indians.

Antiques Galore.
Jim and Irma Terry, owners of Terry's Antiques in Quanah, are happy to provide information on the region. Their collection of wooden Indians is one of the largest in the country.

Cynthia returned to relatives in Texas but her sons grew into warriors. One of those was Quanah, a chief in the "antelope-eaters" segment of the tribe. As the whites moved into West Texas and other chiefs and their nomadic bands were either killed or captured by the army, Quanah continued to harass the invaders whenever and wherever he could. Not until 1875 did he finally surrender, along with 100 warriors and 300 women and children. The U.S. Army and the Texas Rangers breathed a collective sigh of relief.

In later years, Parker became a close friend of President Theodore Roosevelt and often negotiated with the government on the subject of Indian rights. He also adjudicated disputes among his own people, even arresting lawbreakers and delivering them to the white man's justice when necessary. When he died in 1911, he was buried next to his mother, Cynthia, at Fort Sill, Oklahoma. The inscription on his red granite headstone reads: *Resting here until day breaks, and Shadows fall, and darkness disappears, is Quanah Parker, Last Chief of the Comanches.*

Copper Breaks State Park

I left US 287 (with a carved wooden Indian tied to the top of my motorhome) at Quanah, and turned south of SR 6 to see Copper Breaks State Park. Located eleven miles south of town and comprised of about 2,000 acres of juniper breaks and grass-covered mesas, the park offers a sixty-acre fishing lake, a thirty-five-site RV campground with shelters, and several miles of hiking trails.

All Alone with the Wind.
Eleven miles south of the town of Quanah, the 2,000-acre Copper Breaks State Park offers several miles of hiking trails, a fishing lake, and a large RV campground.

Even on weekends, don't be surprised if yours is the only RV in the camping area. The ranger told me that Copper Breaks is far enough away from major centers of population to escape the weekend crush of "getaway" residents, and that he often gets lonely sitting in the middle of 2,000 acres with nothing to do. I didn't spend the night, but the park certainly beckoned me to return. The cool, quiet little lake here is open for swimming as well as fishing, and a dip in the inviting pool would have been a pleasant finale to my long day's drive.

Caprock Canyons State Park

Leaving the park's immaculate campgrounds for another time, however, I returned to SR 6 and followed it south to its junction with US 70. There I resumed my journey westward, driving through fields of alfalfa, wheat, and corn, along some of the straightest, most solitary stretches of road in the state.

As far as I could determine, no travelers' parks exist in the 130 miles between Copper Breaks and the town of Quitaque, so if you don't stay at Copper Breaks and don't wish to camp out, you'll have to drive to Caprock Canyons State Park. To get there, turn north on SR 70 at Matador and follow it to its junction with SR 86. The park lies just west of Quitaque on FM 1065, three miles north of the highway.

Caprock Canyons is named for the scenic and rugged 200-mile-long escarpment that separates the western Panhandle tablelands from the flatter, lower plains to the east. If you're a photographer, you'll notice that Mother Nature has been generous in the park. The terrain is absolutely magnificent—a combination of red sandstone and white caliche eroded into deep canyonlands, towering buttes, and steep-sided buttresses. Panoramic views here are stupendous, especially in the evenings when deep shadows highlight the rugged landscape.

Caprock Canyons encompasses 14,000 acres of the escarpment. Park facilities include two spacious RV campgrounds—each site complete with hookups, shelter, and grill—a visitor center and museum, and several miles of hiking trails. I spent two days here, fishing and taking long walks in the backcountry, and I can heartily recommend a visit, at least an overnight stay.

Still Pumping.
A Panhandle windmill still pumps water from deep wells to watering tanks for cattle.

Panhandle-Plains Historical Museum

When I left Caprock Canyons, I followed SR 86 to Tulia, then turned north on I-27 toward Amarillo. The beautiful farm country around Silverton and Tulia teems with pheasant, so I suggest you keep your speed down. These big birds have a bad habit of trying to fly through windshields as they cross the road from one cornfield to another.

In Canyon, Texas, don't bypass the Panhandle-Plains Historical Museum. Without a doubt, this fine exhibit hall has the best display of just about everything west of the Smithsonian in Washington, D.C. The place is a real surprise, hidden away in a farm town of only 11,000 people, but it will take you a full day to see everything inside.

There are eleven major exhibits on the history and culture of the Great Plains at the museum and none should be missed. I've given a short review of each following, but to really understand just how extensive the exhibits are, you'll have to explore the place yourself.

Hall of Texas History   You'll see everything here that contributed to Texas prehistory and history, from Paleozoic fossils to modern political displays.

Paleontology   The dinosaur exhibits in the Paleontology Hall are astonishing. Also on display are remains of Panhandle life forms from primitive ocean dwellers to the first mammals.

Indians of the Southern Plains   This extensive exhibit traces the history of the Comanche, Kiowa, Arapaho, and Cheyenne Indian nations from the 1700s to modern-day reservations.

Pioneer Town   There is a fully reconstructed old-west town here, complete with stores, shops, and school. Several of the old buildings are authentic—moved piece by piece to the museum from their original locations.

Panhandle Oil and Gas   Believe it or not, the oil and gas exhibit displays a full-sized Texas oil well including drilling machinery and tower. Adjacent to the rig is a 1930s gasoline station, showing where and how the final product was marketed.

Galleries of Art   This hall contains both permanent and traveling collections of paintings, sculpture, and photographs from nationally known artists.

Historic Fashions   Here you'll see all types of clothing worn by Texans throughout the state's history. Exhibits range from buckskin to homespun to modern.

Natural History   Displayed in their natural habitats here are most species of plant and animal life found in northwest Texas.

Transportation   Buggies and wagons from the nineteenth century are on display here, as well as classic automobiles from 1900 to 1950.

T-Anchor Ranch House   The T-Anchor Ranch headquarters were built in 1877 and are some of the oldest structures in the Panhandle. The exhibit contains the main ranch house, outbuildings, and the ranch windmill.

Lifelike Displays.
This replica of a chuck wagon and its cowboy cook in the Panhandle-Plains Museum is so lifelike it is difficult to tell it from the real thing.

The Panhandle-Plains Historical Museum is one of the "must-sees" of Texas. It's located a block east of US 87 on Fourth Avenue. (Be sure and take your camera. Many of the exhibits are located near the windows so you won't even need a flash and photographs are permitted.)

Amarillo

Amarillo lies sixteen miles north of Canyon on I-27. Founded in 1887 by railroad construction gangs, it's the largest and most active city in the Panhandle. Traffic is usually heavy and the streets aren't well marked, but there are some interesting things to see and do so clench your teeth and come anyway.

Make your first stop the Don Harrington Discovery Center on Steit Drive. Attractions in this fifty-acre park include a large aquarium exhibit, a planetarium, a giant kaleidoscope, and all sorts of hands-on displays. It's a great place for kids, but you'll generally see just as many adults.

The Amarillo Art Center on the campus of Amarillo College is a magnificent three-building complex devoted to the fine arts, music, and drama.

For a different experience, visit the world's largest livestock auction, held Monday and Tuesday throughout the year at the Western Stockyards at 100 South Manhattan.

One place you should *not* go in the Amarillo area is Alibates National Monument, where ancient flint quarries are preserved, located about forty-five miles northeast of the city. Described in several guidebooks as a "point of interest," the place may sound interesting, but believe me, it's not. Alibates is closed about ninety percent of the time, and you must make reservations to visit. There's no sign at the entrance road advising

A Crop of Cadillacs.
These car "sculptures" are part of the exhibits at Amarillo's Cadillac Ranch.

Amarillo Chamber of Commerce

you of that fact, however, and the ten miles of unmarked, chuckhole-filled road into monument headquarters will make the most even-tempered RVer scream in frustration.

Palo Duro Canyon State Park

Amarillo offers a good selection of clean, quiet traveler's parks, but I chose to stay instead at Palo Duro Canyon State Park. Located sixteen miles east of Canyon on SR 217, it is the largest state park in Texas and also one of the most dramatic. Encompassing more than 15,000 acres of rugged canyon country, the place is well worth a visit.

Palo Duro will surprise you. One moment you'll be driving along SR 217 through flat and uninteresting farmland, the next, the world simply drops away. And once below the canyon's thousand-foot walls, things are just as dramatic. Simply stated, Palo Duro is a jumbled moonscape of smoky red earth and stone, carved, eroded, and twisted by eons and elements into what most consider to be the most spectacular natural phenomenon in the state.

There are three spacious RV and travel-trailer campgrounds on the canyon floor, all of them situated in scenic areas and all with water and electricity. Park activities are numerous and varied. There's a riding stable in the canyon, for instance, as well as a miniature train ride. Hiking trails (many of them strenuous) spiderweb along the canyon floor and wildlife abounds. As I pulled into my campsite at Hackberry Campground, the six wild turkeys that had been using my shelter for shade slowly strutted into the nearby brush, advising me in their special way that *I* was the visitor and *they* were the residents.

Wary-eyed and Cautious.
A wild turkey, one of Palo Duro's numerous wild animal inhabitants, steps cautiously from the brush near Hackberry Campground.

Surprise—a Canyon!
At Palo Duro Canyon, one moment visitors are driving through flat and uninteresting farmland, and the next, the world simply drops away.

Hiking the Rimrock.
A lone hiker wanders the edge of Palo Duro Canyon. Views of this spectacular chasm from its rim are magnificent.

Reflections

Later that afternoon, as I slouched on a picnic bench behind my RV watching the Texas sun sink toward the canyon rim, I could only marvel at my experiences during the past six months. All told, I had driven more than 5,000 miles and spoken with virtually hundreds of people (and to paraphrase Will Rogers, I never met one I didn't like). I visited places I hadn't known could exist—in one region picking my way on foot through a landscape so thick a fly could not breathe, while in another driving for hours through terrain so flat and wide it took an eternity simply to look from one horizon to the other.

The one thing I realized most as I sat there on my bench was that Texas, beyond a doubt, had become my favorite state. It has its faults, certainly—tornados, dust storms, devasting summer heat, frightening blizzards, rattlesnakes, and masses of land so desolate even the coyotes and jackrabbits go elsewhere. Yet most of the terrain is lovely and varied—so varied in fact, that with every turn and twist in the road comes a new stimulation to one's composite of senses. "This place exerts a magnetic spell," wrote Owen Wister. "The sky is there above it but not of it. Its being is apart; its climate, its light, its own."

POINTS OF INTEREST: Texas Tour 8

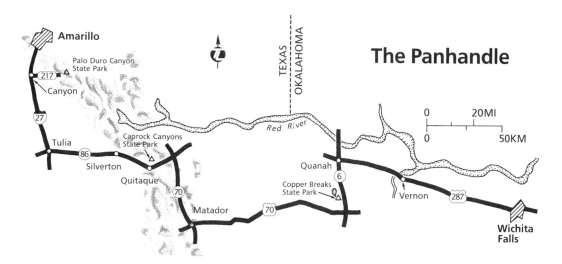

Amarillo
Palo Duro Canyon State Park
217
Canyon
27
Tulia
86
Silverton
Caprock Canyons State Park
Quitaque
70
Matador
70

TEXAS
OKLAHOMA
Red River

The Panhandle

0   20MI
0   50KM

Quanah
6
Copper Breaks State Park
Vernon
287

Wichita Falls

ACCESS: *US 287* west from Wichita Falls.

INFORMATION: *Wichita Falls Texas Tourist Bureau,* 900 Central Freeway, Wichita Falls, TX 76305, (817) 723-7931; *Copper Breaks State Park,* Route 3, Quanah, TX 79252, (817) 839-4331; *Caprock Canyons State Park,* P.O. Box 204, Quitaque, TX 79255, (806) 455-1492; *Panhandle-Plains Historical Museum,* Canyon, TX 79015, (806) 655-7191; *Amarillo Chamber of Commerce,* P.O. Box 9480, Amarillo, TX 79105, (806) 374-1479; *Palo Duro Canyon State Park,* Route 2, Box 285, Canyon, TX 79015, (806) 488-2227.

ANNUAL EVENTS:

Wichita Falls: *Ranch Round-up* (rodeo events performed by cowboys from working Texas ranches, chuck-wagon cook-off, dance) mid-August; *Hotter-Than-Hell 100 Bicycle Ride,* last Saturday in August.

Amarillo: *Cowboy Morning* (chuck-wagon breakfast, rides) June 1–September 15; Palo Duro Canyon State Park; *TEXAS* (spectacular outdoor musical), late June–late August.

MUSEUMS & GALLERIES:

Wichita Falls: *Kell House,* 900 Bluff St., Sunday, 2 P.M.–4 P.M., historic home; *Museum & Art Center,* #2, Eureka Circle, Tuesday through Saturday, 9 A.M.–4:30 P.M., Sunday, 1 P.M.–5 P.M., art and history exhibits.

Vernon: *Red River Valley Museum,* Regional Junior College campus, Tuesday–Sunday, 1 P.M.–5 P.M., archaeological and historical exhibits.

Amarillo: *Amarillo Art Center,* 2200 Van Buren St., Tuesday–Friday, 10 A.M.–5 P.M., Sunday, 1 P.M.–5 P.M., fine arts; *Harrington House,* 1600 South Polk St., advance reservations necessary, neo-classical furnishings.

RESTAURANTS:

Wichita Falls: *McBride's,* 501 Scott St., American-style dining; *Uncle Lynn's Catfish Restaurant,* Hwy. 287 South at Wilson Rd. Exit, family-style meals.

Amarillo: *The Big Texan,* 7301 I-40 (Lakeside exit), steakhouse with family-style dining.

Index

Page numbers in **boldface** refer to illustrations in the text.